Dot.compradors

Political Economy and Development

Published in association with the International Initiative for Promoting Political Economy (IIPPE)

Edited by
Ben Fine (SOAS, University of London)
Dimitris Milonakis (University of Crete)

Political economy and the theory of economic and social development have long been fellow travellers, sharing an interdisciplinary and multidimensional character. Over the last 50 years, mainstream economics has become totally formalistic, attaching itself to increasingly narrow methods and techniques at the expense of other approaches. Despite this narrowness, neoclassical economics has expanded its domain of application to other social sciences, but has shown itself incapable of addressing social phenomena and coming to terms with current developments in the world economy.

With world financial crises no longer a distant memory, and neoliberalism and postmodernism in retreat, prospects for political economy have strengthened. It allows constructive liaison between the dismal and other social sciences and rich potential in charting and explaining combined and uneven development.

The objective of this series is to support the revival and renewal of political economy, both in itself and in dialogue with other social sciences. Drawing on rich traditions, we invite contributions that constructively engage with heterodox economics, critically assess mainstream economics, address contemporary developments, and offer alternative policy prescriptions.

Also available:

The Political Economy of Development: The World Bank, Neoliberalism and Development Research
Edited by Kate Bayliss, Ben Fine and Elisa Van Waeyenberge

Theories of Social Capital: Researchers Behaving Badly
Ben Fine

DOT.COMPRADORS

Power and Policy in the Development of the Indian Software Industry

Jyoti Saraswati

PlutoPress
www.plutobooks.com

First published 2012 by Pluto Press
345 Archway Road, London N6 5AA

www.plutobooks.com

Distributed in the United States of America exclusively by
Palgrave Macmillan, a division of St Martin's Press LLC,
175 Fifth Avenue, New York, NY 10010

British Library Cataloguing in Publication Data
A catalogue record for this book is available from the British Library.

ISBN   978 0 7453 3266 6   Hardback
ISBN   978 0 7453 3265 9   Paperback
ISBN   978 1 8496 4734 2   PDF eBook
ISBN   978 1 8496 4736 6   Kindle eBook
ISBN   978 1 8496 4735 9   EPUB eBook

Library of Congress Cataloging in Publication Data applied for

This book is printed on paper suitable for recycling and made from fully managed
and sustained forest sources. Logging, pulping and manufacturing processes are
expected to conform to the environmental standards of the country of origin.

10   9   8   7   6   5   4   3   2   1

Designed and produced for Pluto Press by Chase Publishing Services Ltd
Typeset from disk by Stanford DTP Services, Northampton, England
Simultaneously printed digitally by CPI Antony Rowe, Chippenham, UK and
Edwards Bros in the United States of America

In memory of Professor S.K. Saraswati

Dot.com *adj.* of or relating to the information technology industry, particularly those aspects most closely associated with the internet and communications technologies.

Comprador *n.* a native-born agent employed by a foreign business to serve as a collaborator or intermediary in commercial transactions.

Contents

Preface

The Indian software industry has been one of the great developmental success stories of the early twenty-first century. Over the past two decades it has evolved from a relatively obscure industry on the margins of the Indian economy to a \$90 billion business and national flagship. This is an impressive achievement in and of itself. But the rate and scale of its growth is only the tip of the iceberg. India now boasts more local firms achieving the Capability Maturity Model (CMM) Level 5 certification – the global standard for high-quality software services provision – than any other nation. And in an industry infamous for oligopoly, it has managed to spawn several national software giants, including Infosys, identified by the *Financial Times* as one of the world's top IT companies (and one of only two non-US firms in the top ten). A comparison with China demonstrates further just how remarkable is India's software success. At the turn of the millennium, the government in Beijing, casting envious glances at software developments in India, announced that it would prioritise the promotion of a globally oriented software services industry. Accordingly, the Chinese state embarked on one of its most ambitious development projects to date, with the objective of replicating and surpassing the industry in India within ten years. A decade later, however, the gulf between the two industries, in both size and sophistication, had widened further, much to the chagrin of the Chinese Communist Party and the bafflement of many of its leading bureaucrats.

The key argument laid out in this book is that these spectacular achievements have resulted in an attitude of complacency towards the Indian software industry amongst observers and analysts alike. Given the facilitating role of the state in the industry's rapid development through the 1990s and the early years of the twenty-first century, the vast majority of commentators have come to the conclusion that current IT policy is in the hands of highly competent bureaucrats. Such faith in these bureaucrats has meant that the recent travails of the industry – the significant slowdown in development overall and the precipitous drop in growth of India's leading software firms in particular – have not received due attention. Instead, there has been an acceptance at face value of the official line that both trends are directly related to the global economic downturn and, therefore, are fleeting. Once the world economy picks up, the consensus view holds, the industry will return to rapid growth and development.

By adopting a political economy approach to the industry's development, the book paints a less sanguine picture. In particular, three original, and related, observations are put forward, highlighting how misplaced is the faith in both the bureaucrats and the industry's future. First, the bureaucrats involved in IT strategy are shown to be neither highly competent nor omniscient. Instead, they have been guilty of blindly following policy diktats determined by pressures and interests emanating both from within the industry and from the wider political economy. Far from being policy innovators, they appear merely to be engaged in the grunt work of implementing IT policy devised by their vested-interest masters. Second, it is argued that as a result of the industry's rate and pattern of growth, as well as wider changes to the country's political economy and ideological climate, the National Association of Software and Service Companies (NASSCOM) has become the most powerful of these vested interests, with commensurate influence over the form and direction of IT policy. Third, it is contended that in the last decade a small clique of Western firms have established de facto control over NASSCOM, and through NASSCOM, over IT policy. Wisely, this clique has populated the association's upper echelons with Indian 'yes-men' – the eponymous 'dot.compradors' – to retain the appearance of a national character, while pushing forward a policy agenda based on their narrow, short-term commercial interests. Significantly, this agenda also happens to be hugely detrimental to the short-term needs of the Indian software firms and, equally, the long-term health of the nation's software industry. The arguments offered here suggest that it is these factors, not the global economic downturn, which is at the root of the industry's slowing growth.

While the book should be essential reading for all those working in, or on, the India software industry, it will also appeal to a much wider audience. First, due to its alternative, political economy account of the industry's evolution, it will be of prime interest for scholars, students and practitioners of development. In particular, by examining the hard realities and trade-offs in industrial policymaking, it will be of use to critics and advocates of state intervention alike. In addition, by providing a very different version of the industry's development from that found in World Bank reports, the book provides policymakers with an alternative view of the possibilities and pitfalls of utilising information technology (IT) to foster growth in the developing world.

Second, the book will be of use to academics, policymakers and politicians critical of the evolving economic and political system in India. In particular, by undermining the neo-liberal interpretation of the industry's development – a central ideological pillar and rhetorical device for advocates pushing for greater liberalisation – the book provides a powerful counter-argument and alternative narrative in favour of more, not less, state intervention.

Third, as a result of its analysis of the current and unfolding events in the industry, the book serves as a primer for business people considering founding a software start-up in India, outsourcing services to an Indian software firm, or establishing a subsidiary in the country. It does so by offering more than the standard clichés and tropes attached to the industry.

Finally, it is hoped that the book's accessible style of writing will ensure that those with a passing, rather than professional, interest in IT or India will find it engaging and informative. It separates fact from fiction in the 'India Shining' accounts, explains how a high-tech industry can develop in a poor country, and provides an indication of where the industry, and India more broadly, might be heading over the next decade.

Acknowledgements

The book has its genesis in my doctoral research at the Department of Economics, School of Oriental and African Studies, University of London, started half a decade ago. The lengthy gestation of the book means that I have been fortunate enough to have benefitted from the help, support and advice of a large number of friends, colleagues, students and family. Of these, I am particularly grateful to Professor Ben Fine for his expert supervision during my Ph.D. and support afterwards. Without his words of advice and guidance this book would not have been possible. I would also like to thank the Pluto team for their assistance, in particular Roger van Zwanenberg and David Shulman, and Anthony Winder, who did a marvellous job with the copy-editing.

In addition, I wish to extend my gratitude to Dr Sonali Deraniyagala and Ashok Mitra who have both provided commentary on the Ph.D. as it progressed. I am also thankful to Dr Ha-Joon Chang and Professor Alfredo Saad-Filho, who provided a rigorous testing of my arguments at the Ph.D. viva, as well as Professor Barbara Harriss-White and Professor Ray Kiely for many useful discussions on the topic. A thank you too to Professors Peter Evans, Vibha Pingle, Suma Athreye, Richard Heeks and Anthony D'Costa, for sharing their insights on the Indian IT industry with me.

Other persons from academia, the media and the Indian software services industry whose insights have helped in the writing of this book include the following: Dimitra Petroupolou, Chirashri Dasgupta, Radha Upadhya, Jan Knorich, Sobhi Samour, Ramesh Sangaralingam, Ajay Gambhir, Nivirkar Singh, Abir Mukherjee, Neeraj Bhardwaj, Darren Sharma, Dan Breznitz, Ananth Durai, Rajiv Malhotra, Anindita Bose, Stefan Lang, Michael Wyn-Williams, Tom Luff, Bryan Mabee, Rick Saull, Jossey Matthews, Tim Wright, Tom Barnes, Grace Guest, Neil Dutta, Dev Maitra, Srimonto Das, Hazel Gray, Indraneel Sircar, Jim O'Neill, Gautam Chakraborty, Daniela Tavasci, Shub Sarker, Hugo Dobson, Yossi Mekelberg, Sahar Rad, Humam Al-Jazeeri and Kuton Chakraborty.

I would also like to extend my appreciation to the students I taught at Oxford University, New York University and Queen Mary, University of London, whose interest in the character of Indian development in the twenty-first century spurred me on to write a book on the topic that was accessible not just to a small group of academics but to the wider public.

And finally, special thanks to my mother and my wife, for all their love and support.

Jyoti Saraswati
London, September 2011

A Note on the Terminology

The IT industry is highly fluid in terms of its structures, operations, processes and dominant firms for a number of reasons. Companies once engaged in computer manufacturing have forayed, and even shifted wholesale, into new operational and commercial lines within the industry. The most well-known example of this is IBM, which transformed itself within a decade from a firm whose core operation was computer manufacture to a company primarily engaged in the provision of IT consultancy. HP now appears to be following suit. There has also been the expansion by IT firms – via mergers, acquisitions and organic growth – into non-IT-related industries (and vice versa), blurring the very borders of the industry. IBM again provides an excellent example: not only is it the world's leading software services firm, it is also one of the premier providers of management consultancy. Underpinning such fluidity are the successive waves of what the great Austrian economist Joseph Schumpeter referred to as 'creative destruction', the industry upheavals wrought by technological breakthroughs.

Such fluidity in the industry translates into the never-ending introduction of new firms, terms and concepts in the industry terminology and jargon. Even more troubling than the rapidity of new terms is that many of the outdated terms and concepts do not immediately disappear but survive in an undead state, disregarded by those within the industry but still prevalent in public discourse for years and even decades afterwards. Thus, across countries, historical periods, firms, industries and even classes, the same term (for example the IT Industry) can have multiple usages (it may or may not include semiconductors, IT-enabled services, etc.); and one operation (for example the writing of customised software) can be referred to using different terms (IT services, software services, etc.).

For the author of a book intended to be sold internationally and to be of value to industry insiders and informed public alike, such a situation poses a significant challenge. Much thought has gone into choosing which terms and which meanings will be employed. The terms selected for this book are those with the greatest ability to facilitate understanding. They have been based on the following criteria: their usage and awareness globally in order to permit recognition; their descriptive value in order to aid inference and recollection; their specificity in order to facilitate analysis and avoid conflation and confusion with other terms; and their presentation, avoiding too many prefixes, suffixes and acronyms, in order to enhance readability and engagement.

The terms selected are not going to find favour amongst everyone, particularly those more au fait with alternative terms. This is inevitable given the situation of the same term having multiple usages or the same operation being referred to by multiple terms. The best that can be done is to be clear at the outset regarding the meaning attached to the terms used in the book (see Glossary) and to be consistent in their usage.

Glossary

Back-Office Operations
A subset of a firm's non-core business processes. The term incorporates all the firm's operations which take place 'behind the scenes' such as data entry, accounting and human resources. They can be provided by third party contractors as part of business process outsourcing services.

Bangalored
A neologism used to describe the offshoring or outsourcing of software production (and jobs) from the West to developing country locales.

Body-shopping
The business model in which software firms send employees to the client's headquarters to provide software services. While remote delivery of services has reduced the need and practice of body-shopping, it is still required at the beginning and end of software projects.

Bundling
The process by which computer manufacturers sell computers with software already installed. By doing so, the market for software services provision is often reduced.

Business Houses
India's major industrial conglomerates. They are a specific and highly influential fraction of Indian capital. Depending on the criteria adopted, there are between ten and twenty Business Houses. They are usually family based, with origins dating back to the nineteenth century.

Business Process Outsourcing (BPO) Services
The provision of a corporation's non-core business processes by a third party contractor, usually a software services firm. Business processes that are often outsourced include both back office and front desk operations. In this book business process outsourcing services will be considered a subset of the software services industry.

Captive

The term 'captive' is used to describe TNC subsidiaries based in India engaged in software production and services (including IT-enabled services) primarily for export with little or no linkages with the rest of the domestic economy.

Compound Annual Growth Rate (CAGR)

The year-over-year growth rate of an industry's revenues, exports or other development indicators.

Comprador

An individual of, and in, a developing country who serves Western interests. Such service is usually, though not always, implicit. Moreover, the rationale for such service is material gain rather than ideological or political conviction.

Computer

An electronic machine for storing, retrieving and analysing information.

Computer Hardware

The mechanical, magnetic, electronic and electrical components of a computer.

Computer Hardware Industry

The industry involved in the manufacture and assembly of computers (the computer industry for short).[1]

Computer Hardware Installed Base

The number and character (that is, bundled or unbundled) of computers in operation in any particular country.

Department of Electronics (DoE)

A government body established in India in the early 1970s to design and implement IT policy. In 2004, due to the redrawing of bureaucratic lines, it became the Department of Information Technology within the Ministry of Information Technology and Communications. For the sake of continuity, the book will refer to the DoE throughout.

'Developmental Department' Literature (DDL)

The term used in this book to refer to the academic literature that portrays the Department of Electronics as a 'developmental department', i.e. an autonomous, developmentally inclined government body within the wider Indian political economy.

Front-Desk Operations

A subset of a firm's non-core business processes. The term embraces all operations which require interaction with the firm's customers or clients. These include, most prominently, call centres engaged in customer service and sales.

Global Giants

A specific fraction of capital attached to the software services industry, comprising the four major corporations that dominate the highest tier of software services. These firms are IBM, EDS (recently renamed HP Enterprise Services), Accenture and Cap Gemini.

Import Substitution Industrialisation (ISI)

An economic policy agenda centred on the replacement of imports with domestically produced goods.

Infant Industry Protection

A strategy of development by which the state provides trade protection to domestic firms with the aim that this will help firms to expand rapidly and mature commercially.

Information Technology (IT)

The general term to describe the whole science of computing, transmitting data from place to place, and techniques for handling information.[2]

Intermediate Class

A specific fraction of capital in India politically influential throughout the 1960s and 1970s. This class was engaged in the petty production of consumer goods and lobbied for extensive controls to prevent Business House encroachment into such sectors.

IT-enabled Services (ITES)

Services which are delivered using advances in IT and telecommunications technology. The most prominent example of an IT-enabled service is customer support via call centres. IT-enabled services can be provided in-house by a firm or via an outside contractor through business process outsourcing services.

IT Industry

The entire panoply of the digital processing, storage and communication of information. The IT industry is normally divided between the software and hardware industries, but in this book will also include IT-enabled services (ITES) provided by 'captives' and firms providing business process outsourcing services.[3]

Licensing

A strategy of development by which firms are only allowed to produce certain goods and services if they have a government licence. Licences for industries are usually limited in number, allowing in theory for the most effective utilisation of scarce resources and avoiding unnecessary duplication.

Majors

The largest three Indian software firms: TCS, Infosys and Wipro. These three firms are responsible for generating nearly 50 per cent of India's software services exports and over 25 per cent of the total revenues of the Indian IT industry.[4] Until recently they appeared poised to break the oligopoly of the Global Giants in the highest echelons of software services.

National Association of Software and Service Companies (NASSCOM)

The business association of the Indian software services industry. It is regarded as the voice of the industry and is also chief purveyor of data on the industry.

National Champions

Large, export-oriented firms with close relations to their home state and operating in key strategic and/or industrial sectors.

Non-resident Indian (NRI)

An Indian citizen who resides permanently outside India.

Offshoring

The process by which a firm shifts part or all of its production process to another country but maintains production in-house. This usually occurs for one or more of the following reasons: to access cheaper and/or better skilled labour; to access other inputs such as materials; and proximity to major markets.

Outsourcing

As defined by the British Computer Society, outsourcing is 'the purchase of services from outside contractors rather than employing staff to do the tasks'.[5] This is usually carried out for one or more of the following reasons: to reduce costs; to improve the quality of the service; or to allow for specialisation.

Poaching

The practice by which firms 'tap up' and lure away employees from other companies. For the software services industry, in which retention of employees is crucial for firm development, poaching can undermine attempts at migrating up the value-chain.

Small and Medium-Sized Enterprises (SMEs)
Firms whose revenues or employee numbers fall below certain limits. In India, firms having revenues falling below $2 million are generally regarded as SMEs.

Software
The set of instructions which are used to direct the computer to carry out operations which are wanted by the user.[6]

Software Industry
The industry involved in writing and producing software. It is typically divided between firms in the software package industry and those in the software services industry. In this book 'captives' providing in-house software services (including IT-enabled services) for their parent companies will also fall under the software industry's umbrella.

Software Package Industry
The industry involved in the production of software in standardised form for general sale to large numbers of users.

Software Services Industry[7]
The industry involved in the production of software as a service for a single specific user. This ranges from the design of highly complex IT systems for corporations and governments to basic data processing. The industry can be divided into three tiers: IT consultancy, IT services and IT outsourcing (which includes business process outsourcing services).

Software Services Firms (SSFs)
Firms engaged in one or more of the three tiers of the software services industry. The key software services firms are the four Global Giants and the three Indian Majors.

Transnational Corporation (TNC)
A corporation which produces goods and/or services in more than one country.

Transnational Computer Corporation (TNCC)
A corporation which manufactures computers in more than one country. While most computer manufacturers are now transnational computer corporations, during the 1970s it was a useful term to distinguish between computer firms whose production was centred

exclusively in one country and the usually much larger computer firms operating internationally.

Useful Idiots
Persons who are manipulated by vested interests to carry out actions which they believe to be in their own direct self-interest but which are, in practice, the exact opposite.

Value Chain
Interlinked value-adding activities within the process which converts inputs into outputs.

A Primer: The Seven Leading Myths about the Indian Software Industry

'Bangalore: India's Silicon City'; 'Bangalore and Job Cuts Galore'; 'The Bill Gates of Bangalore';[1]

As evidenced by the above headlines, the southern Indian city of Bangalore is now synonymous with software services in much the same way as the US city of Detroit was once tied to the manufacture of automobiles and the French region of Champagne still is with the production of sparkling wine. Moreover, and unlike Detroit or Champagne, such a profile has been established extremely rapidly. As late as 1990 Bangalore was still referred to locally as a 'pensioners' paradise', its pleasant climate, spacious bungalows and sedate atmosphere attracting India's affluent elderly; outside of India it was virtually unknown. By 2010, all this had changed: it had become the world's second-fastest-growing metropolis after Shanghai and internationally renowned as Asia's 'Silicon Valley'.[2] Whereas only a decade ago any Western leader visiting India would stop only in New Delhi, it has now become customary first to visit Bangalore to pay respect to the city perceived as the embodiment of India's rapidly growing economy.

In July 2010 it was the turn of the prime minister of the country that had played a major part in establishing Bangalore as a 'pensioners' paradise' to pay homage to its remarkable transformation.[3] Speaking at the headquarters of Infosys, one of India's leading software firms, the British prime minister, David Cameron, referred glowingly to Bangalore as 'the city that symbolises India's reawakening'. Not to be outdone, the French president, Nicholas Sarkozy, in a speech to Indian scientists at the Indian Space Research Organisation in Bangalore five months later, referred to the city, with typical Gallic ebullience, as the 'world capital of computer services'. Even as far back as 2004, Senator John Kerry, then in the running to be US president, in a major breach of US political protocol, implored Americans to learn from foreigners. The foreigners in question were Bangaloreans, and the practice to be emulated was their embrace of information technology.[4]

Myth 1: The city of Bangalore is the hub of the Indian software industry.

Such lavish praise meted out by a long line of global leaders is odd, given that Bangalore is not even India's major software hub, let alone the global centre of information technology, as many seem to believe.[5] Chennai, Mumbai and New Delhi can all lay far greater claim to being the heart of India's software services industry. For example, there are more software firms in both Mumbai (149) and New Delhi (156) than in Bangalore (126).[6] Moreover, software firms in Mumbai are responsible for a far greater share of the industry's revenues (32 per cent) than those in Bangalore (24 per cent).[7] In terms of technical sophistication and greatest productivity, the software firms located in Chennai lead the way.[8]

The fixation on Bangalore is just one example of how the common Western perception of the Indian IT industry differs substantially from the reality on the ground. The hyperbole attached to Bangalore can be explained primarily by the fact that the majority of Western TNCs establishing IT-related subsidiaries in India have selected Bangalore as their destination of choice.[9] Over 40 per cent of IT-related firms in Bangalore were foreign subsidiaries. In contrast, foreign subsidiaries account for only 24 per cent of IT-related firms in Mumbai and just 16 per cent in Chennai. In other words, from the perspective of Western firms, Bangalore looms larger than any other Indian city as a software base. However, as TNCs generate only a small part of the Indian IT industry's revenues, Bangalore's contribution to it is limited. Thus, from an India perspective, Bangalore is no more important as a software base than Chennai, New Delhi or Mumbai, and arguably less so.[10]

Whereas the global media's focus on Bangalore can be understood as a simple mistake based on a particular vantage point, this is not necessarily the case with other erroneous understandings of the industry. It would not be an overstatement to say that some books, reports and articles on the industry have provided a view so distorted, at times even inverted, that they invite the accusation of being more akin to Orwellian 'Newspeak' than representative of fact.[11] In other words, the various features of the industry propagated by the mainstream media have not so much been innocently misconstrued through a series of blunders and misunderstandings as deliberately constructed (or, more accurately, misconstructed) in order to serve a politico-ideological agenda. With this in mind, six other widely believed myths regarding the Indian software industry will be refuted below so as to clear the reader's mind of any existing prejudices before embarking on the main body of the book.

Myth 2: The Indian software industry primarily consists of call centres.

Ask anyone in the West what they think of when they hear of the 'Indian IT industry' or 'Indian software industry' and the vast majority of them will say 'call centres'.[12] However, the notion that the Indian software industry *is* a call-centre industry is entirely wrong. Of course, a call-centre industry does exist in India, and has expanded rapidly over the past decade. But the revenues of the software industry in India are still primarily generated through higher-end software services.[13] While the call-centre industry has witnessed high rates of growth, it still constitutes less than a third of the entire revenues of the industry.

But then why are so few people outside of India aware of the higher-end component of the software industry?

It has nothing to do with a relatively greater orientation of Indian call centres to Western markets. Both Indian call centres and higher-end software services provision are primarily export-oriented. In fact, most people living outside of India are likely to use software written by Indians working in India for Indian firms far more frequently than they would an Indian call centre. For example, text someone from a mobile phone and it is likely you will be using software designed by Wipro, a major Indian software firm. Take a flight on an Airbus plane and the pilot will be using software designed by HCL, another company from India. Even the London underground, the embodiment of past British engineering feats, is now run by software designed by the Indian firm CMC.

The key reason for a lack of awareness regarding the ubiquity of Indian software would appear to be the manner in which higher-end software services are delivered. For example, a Western caller to a call centre in India is immediately able to infer, from the accent and name of the call-centre employee, that the call centre is in India.[14] In stark contrast, given the intangible and invisible nature of the delivery of higher-end software services, the Western user of such a service would probably have no idea of where and by whom it was written. So as most Westerners' only *knowing* contact with the Indian software industry is via a call centre, their natural conclusion is that the industry consists solely of call centres.

This view is further reinforced by the Western media's fascination with Indian call centres. This has already spawned a popular British comedy series, *Mumbai Calling*, and an eminently forgettable Hollywood film, *Outsourced*. More substantively, almost every BBC or CNN news clip purporting to cover the 'Indian IT industry' or 'Indian software industry' invariably shows images of people answering phones in call centres rather than writing software code.[15] Documentaries too, have shown a preference for call-centre coverage. Take, for example, an episode of the US television series *30 Days*, in which the protagonist was a former IBM software engineer in the United States who had recently been made redundant (or, to use the neologism, 'bangalored') by IBM's offshoring of software jobs to India. According to the show's premise and voice-over, the engineer was going to travel to India and live and work 'with the person who had taken his job'. However, instead of joining up with an IBM middle manager, he found himself with a fresh-faced college graduate in a training school for people wanting to work in call centres. The reason appears to be sheer entertainment – there is simply more mileage in coverage of call-centre training (usually involving eager young Indians grappling with US slang, sayings and soap operas) than of the design of applications software.

Myth 3: Foreign direct investment has played a key role in the development of the industry.

People assume that the Indian software industry was initiated by foreign IT corporations investing in India and that it still primarily comprises the subsidiaries of foreign firms (referred to as 'captives' in India). This reflects a tendency in Western academic and media circles first to identify a link between any successful industry in the developing world and the West and then to emphasise and exaggerate the positive role this connection has played.[16] For example, US semiconductor giant Texas Instruments (TI), the first TNC to establish a software development subsidiary in India, is typically credited with being the 'earliest harbinger of a more widespread IT expansion' in India.[17]

However, the real effect of foreign direct investment (FDI) and TNCs in the Indian software industry, and the IT industry more broadly, is very different.

First and foremost, the current influx of FDI and the scaling up of TNC captives in India is not the cause of the industry's growth but, rather, an outcome of its success.[18] The influx has only occurred over the past decade, and was primarily prompted by a realisation amongst the Global Giants (most notably IBM) that they needed to scale up operations in India in order to compete with the rapidly emerging Indian software firms (see Chapter 8).

Second, despite the hyperbole attached to the influx of IT-related FDI into India, their effect on revenue growth remains negligible. The vast majority of the industry's revenues are generated by Indian software firms, particularly the largest. Moreover, as the captives of foreign corporations are primarily engaged in lower-skilled call-centre work and other forms of ITES, the higher-end software services work exported from India to the rest of the world is almost exclusively from local firms.[19]

Third, far from being saviours and catalysts, foreign corporations have tended to act as a fetter on the Indian IT industry's development rather than as its initiator.[20] This accusation can be most effectively levelled against foreign computer manufacturers operating in India in the 1960s and 1970s (see Chapter 5).[21] However, it can also be increasingly applied to the activities of TNC captives now operating in India (see Chapter 8).

Myth 4: The Indian diaspora in the United States has played a major role in the development of the Indian software industry.

The Indian community in the United States is the wealthiest, most professionalised and best educated of all major ethnic groups in the country (including non-Hispanic white Americans) (see www. census.gov). Their economic contribution to the US economy has been immense. According to some literature, they have also played a key role in the Indian economy too, particularly through fostering the growth of the Indian IT industry.

There are two main roles the Indian diaspora in the United States are alleged to have played. The first is as promoters. For example, TI's decision to invest in India is often attributed to the leading talent in their US headquarters being of Indian origin. This, it is argued, prompted TI to 'go where the talent was'.[22] Their second role is that of entrepreneurs. Indians who had emigrated to the United States in the 1970s and 1980s to work for US firms are allegedly now returning to India to establish their own software firms.[23] This phenomenon has been referred to as the 'inverse brain drain' or 'brain gain', with the assumption that such returning entrepreneurs are not only boosting the industry's revenues, but also bringing with them a whole array of business skills.[24]

However, there are a number of problems with the notion of the Indian diaspora playing such a positive, facilitative role in the development of the Indian software industry.

First, the emigration of much of India's intellectual talent which has resulted in its huge diaspora has been and continues to be a major impediment to the development of local technical capabilities and a strain on educational resources.[25] Second, the much touted returnees are more a trickle than a cascade, especially when compared to the continued exodus from India to the United States.[26] Third, far from being entrepreneurial dynamos, returning members of the Indian diaspora are primarily sent back to India by their employers – US TNCs – to manage those firms' Indian subsidiaries.[27] This is borne out by the figures: despite the thousands of returnees, software firms established by returning Indians are said to number only around 200.[28]

Myth 5: The Indian software services industry is a recent phenomenon brought about by the twin advances of breakthroughs in telecommunications technology and the country's economic liberalisation.

In general, people perceive the Indian software industry as a relatively new phenomenon, emerging in the 1990s during the era of 'globalisation'. This stems in part from the very nature of the industry as it is now – transnational and high-tech – as well as the visual hints emanating from the futuristic steel-and-glass buildings which house the world's top software services firms, both Indian and foreign. It is also the result of a strong bias within the majority of literature on the industry that takes India's economic liberalisation in 1991 as an analytical starting point, assuming that the preceding period has little, if any, relevance to understanding the current structure and dynamics of the software services industry.

Yet the roots of the industry hark back to an Indian government report in the late 1960s entitled *Computers in India*, which noted that 'software development would seem to have a very high employment potential in a country like India'. This was followed by the Software Export Scheme of 1972, which aimed to establish a software export industry in India.[29] Within two years Indian firms were exporting software, solely due to the scheme's support. The importance of the scheme, alongside the longevity of the industry, is evidenced by the fact that four of the five largest Indian software firms in 2010 have their roots in the 1970s.[30]

Myth 6: Indian IT policy is being formulated by dedicated, autonomous technocrats with mid-to-long-term perspectives.

The Department of Electronics (DoE), which is ostensibly responsible for IT policy, has received a great deal of praise in academic literature on the Indian software industry. The personnel who work in the department have been venerated as 'policy entrepreneurs' and 'enlightened bureaucrats'.[31] The IT policies they have pursued since the late 1970s have been deemed 'developmental' and even 'visionary'. However, the glow in which these bureaucrats currently bask is more jaundiced than haloed.

While policy minutiae have proliferated, bureaucrats within the DoE have failed to acknowledge the contradictions between one policy and another as well as to situate the industry in its broader social and political conditions.[32] Success is defined in quantitative terms of revenues and growth rates rather than structural changes and productivity. Discussions over the dynamics, trends and patterns of growth in the industry have been fastidiously avoided. As a result, there is a distinct absence of any overarching economic or political strategy aimed at the sustainable growth of the industry. Instead, policy documents are filled with buzzwords lacking clarity and economic targets based on simplistic extrapolations.

Even more concerning than the absence of rigorous, intellectual effort is evidence that the DoE appears to have been captured by special interests. A cursory comparison of DoE literature with that produced and published by the National Association of Software and Service Companies (NASSCOM) suggests that the much-feted 'policy entrepreneurs' have abdicated (or should that be outsourced?) policymaking to the entrepreneurs, the industry association and their favoured consultant, McKinsey.

The outcome of this has been negative in two ways. First, issues which do not directly affect the dominant interests within NASSCOM but are of vital importance for the industry's long-term development are not even raised, let alone addressed, by current policy. Second, this has allowed every policy promoted by NASSCOM to be translated directly into practice, no matter how detrimental that may be to the sustainability of the industry and how great an impediment it may be to the wider development of the country.

Myth 7: The software industry's growth represents an unequivocal good for the country.

It is widely assumed that the Indian software industry is an unequivocal good for the country. On a superficial basis this appears to make perfect sense, and a voluminous literature exists citing the various positive effects on the Indian economy induced by the industry.

Employment generation is prominent in the discourse. It is often pointed out that in addition to generating millions of jobs directly through its rapid growth, the industry – via expenditure on construction, transportation and catering – has generated many more jobs indirectly.[33] At the last count, approximately 10 million people were employed, directly or indirectly, as a result of the Indian software industry. Even in a country as populous as India, this job generation is welcome.

Other positive effects have also been identified. Less tangible but no less significant has been the influence of the industry on changing global perceptions of India. NASSCOM claims the industry has played 'a significant role in transforming India's international image from a slow moving bureaucratic economy to a land of innovative entrepreneurs'.[34] The government department responsible for IT policy also acknowledges the positive effect of the industry on global views of India. Using the business jargon which increasingly permeates its reports, the DoE boasts that the industry has given India 'formidable brand equity.'[35] Such international perceptions play a key part in helping Indian firms from all manner of sectors to win contracts and break into export markets, as well as attracting FDI.

The pioneering development economist and Nobel laureate Professor Amartya Sen pinpoints two other positive contributions made by the industry to wider Indian development.[36] The first is its demonstration effect on Indian firms in other sectors. As Sen notes, the software industry has 'inspired Indian industrialists to face the world economy as a potentially big participant, not a tiny bit player'. Second, he detects the industry as instilling a greater respect for technical learning amongst the young. He sees the industry's success as encouraging 'many bright [Indian] students to go technical rather than merely contemplative'. Given that over 30 per cent of the workforce of the industry is female, there is also an emerging literature on the industry's role in reshaping gender relations.[37]

Such positives have, however, to be kept in proportion. Professors C.P. Chandrasekhar and Jayati Ghosh, while accepting the aforementioned contributions, view the industry as an 'exaggerated development opportunity'.[38] They argue that the fruits of the industry's growth are limited to an extremely narrow stratum of Indian society: namely the upper and middle classes. Whether the industry prospers or fails, they argue, the implications for wider Indian development are negligible. The industry is merely a distraction from more significant issues – such as the distribution of land rights, the provision of basic needs, the generation of jobs which pay above subsistence for the masses, and the expansion of industry – which will fundamentally determine whether India becomes a developed country or not.

However, one can go beyond the critique of the panacea myth proffered by Ghosh and Chandrasekhar and argue that the industry's positive contributions to India have been more than balanced out by the negative consequences of its political influence. Three examples provide succour to such a damning perspective.

First, the industry's association, NASSCOM, using its political influence over both the government and most of the major state governments, has successfully 'promoted' two policies which are, indirectly, impeding IT diffusion in the country. These policies are, first, a zealous anti-piracy campaign in software and, second, the use of expensive Microsoft software over free software. The big beneficiary is Microsoft – which, incidentally, sits on the executive council of NASSCOM.[39] However, free software and piracy are the chief mechanisms by which IT diffusion occurs, so these policies have a disastrous negative effect on the spread of IT across India.

The facts and figures speak for themselves. Despite the rhetoric of India being 'amongst the top IT nations',[40] the penetration of IT in India has been abysmal. Despite India having the largest and most advanced software industry not just in the region but in the entire developing world, computer and internet usage is greater in Pakistan, a country more synonymous with international terrorism than with information technology.[41] Indeed, throughout the period during which the software industry in India grew at phenomenal rates, India's world ranking in IT diffusion fell: from an already disgracefully low 105th in 1995, it plummeted to 112th in 2008.[42] Far from this being an odd and perplexing paradox, India's low level of IT penetration is directly rooted in the political economy of the software industry in India.

Second, the industry is playing a role in the stagnation witnessed in other sectors of the Indian economy. For example, using its political influence, it has successfully attracted both the Indian state's energies and its ample investment in infrastructure. And by exercising its leverage over the state, it has also won itself all manner of tax exemptions, meaning that its returns to the state's coffers are minimal. There can be little doubt that the industry is receiving more from the state than it is contributing back. And through gaining such support, it is diverting scarce resources from the sectors which have far greater need for it and whose social and economic returns are significantly higher. It is a case study par excellence in combined and uneven development with an ample dose of unfairness thrown in.

And third, not content with the stagnation, the industry – via NASSCOM – now appears to be proposing that the Indian state sacrifice all other sectors for its continued vitality. The crux of the matter is the issue of US visas for Indian software programmers, which NASSCOM deems to be of prime importance for the continuing development of the industry. The problem for the state is that, to secure the visas that NASSCOM claims the industry requires, it may have to liberalise its agricultural, industrial and financial sectors. This is because at both multilateral and bilateral levels, increased numbers of visas come with the quid pro quo of increased liberalisation elsewhere (see Chapter 10).

To summarise, there was a time when the industry merely reflected the contradictions inherent within Indian development – namely, those arising from a skewed pattern of elitist development. Now, however, using its political influence, it is exacerbating these contradictions by providing greater resources for those already well stocked in privileges, while denying resources to those severely lacking in them. By doing so, it is creating socio-political conditions, such as growing revolutionary activity amongst the most disadvantaged classes in the country, which may well jeopardise its very survival in the medium term. Rather than a panacea for underdevelopment, the industry increasingly appears like a recipe for disaster.

1
Introduction

I write because there is some lie I want to expose, some fact to which I want to draw attention, and my initial concern is to get a hearing.

George Orwell[1]

[The economist] must examine the past, in light of the present, for the purposes of the future.

John Maynard Keynes[2]

1.1 BACKGROUND

Over the past decade the Indian software industry has become all things to all men, ranging from the intellectual periphery of the Occident to the fanatical core of the Subcontinent. Neo-liberals have perceived the industry as evidence that economic liberalisation in India is working.[3] In diametric contrast, statists have pointed to the industry's rapid growth as a demonstration of yet another example of the necessity of state intervention to engender development.[4] For globalisation gurus it epitomises the sidelining of distance as a determinant in the accumulation of capital – often referred to as the 'flat world' phenomenon – while for the Indian middles classes it is the embodiment of a new, dynamic India.[5] Even Hindu nationalists, not known for their embrace of modernity, have jumped on the IT bandwagon, proclaiming the success of the software industry as reflecting the superiority of Indic thinking and culture.[6]

Such stances have been primarily based on either ideology or emotion: to prove an academic theory, confirm a world view or assert one's superiority. Scholars have been guilty, by and large, of a pick-and-mix approach to facts and figures, assembling them according to established views. The academic literature has, therefore, been characterised by an extreme expediency in terms of which evidence is used, abused or discarded. Moreover, given the underlying ideological and political motivations, many such studies have been impelled towards a degree of sensationalism in order to grab attention and penetrate public discourse. As a result, the proliferation of books and articles on the industry has, paradoxically, been accompanied by a rapid deterioration in any substantive knowledge about it.

Like their academic counterparts, well-respected industry commentators in the Indian and international business media have also shown a remarkable lack of interest in the workings of the industry. This is not, however, based on ideological point-scoring. Rather, this can be attributed to an entrenched sense of complacency regarding the current health of the industry and its future development brought on by two decades of virtually uninterrupted double-digit growth. Such spectacular development has created the impression that those responsible for IT policy in India – the bureaucrats and NASSCOM's top brass – are highly competent, and that therefore the industry is in safe hands. This Panglossian attitude has, in turn, rendered unnecessary any independent analysis of IT policy and the situation 'on the ground'.

The combination of academic point-scoring and journalistic credulity has meant that there has been little progress in understanding the *actual* material conditions of the Indian software industry, past, present and evolving.[7] The changes in the underlying structure and economic relations of the industry have been either largely ignored or expediently interpreted; thorough analyses of the commercial linkages within the industry, and between the industry and other sectors, national and international, are rare; and political terms such as vested interests and corruption are virtually absent from the discourse in which commentators and scholars have been dazzled (or should that be blinded?) by the industry's halo.

These deficiencies have taken on greater saliency in light of the industry's rapid slowdown in growth from 2008 onwards. They have ensured that industry commentators and academics have blindly accepted the official line that the precipitous drop in industry growth rates is a result of the international economic downturn, oblivious both to the growing strains in the industry's economic relations and to the fact that the global recession has actually been a boon rather than a curse for software services industries in other countries. The attribution of the industry's slowdown to external causes has also meant that IT policy in India has evaded scrutiny. This has proved highly fortuitous for the policymakers, as even a cursory glance at the state's current interventions would suggest that it is having an adverse effect on the industry's development, in particular that of the major Indian software firms.

1.2 AIMS

There is a touch of farce about the scenario outlined above – less Karl Marx, more Marx Brothers. However, the comedy belies a very concerning situation. If the industry's slowdown in growth is not related to external demand but is instead due to internal structural issues, any international economic upturn is not going to translate smoothly into the revitalisation of the industry. As such, the industry's travails are likely to continue longer than is commonly anticipated. This is especially the case if IT policy is not able to address the problems adequately. Given that current IT policy appears to be fomenting rather than addressing the industry's woes, the omens for the long-term health of the industry are not good.

The key aim of this book is to explicate this imbroglio. However, contemporary analysis of the industry can only make sense and bear fruit if it is combined with a study of its historical development. It is necessary to understand the industry's previous structural changes in order to grasp the transformation it is now undergoing. And it is vital to know the determinants of IT policy over time to identify accurately those that currently shape it. The essential foundation in explaining the Indian software industry's current predicament is, therefore, a detailed, analytical study of its origins and growth over the past four decades. Taking this maxim as point of departure, this book has three specific aims.

- First, to provide a detailed and accurate historical account of the industry's development. More specifically, it will examine how and why the state intervened in different periods and what effects such interventions have had on the industry's structural transformation.
- Second to draw from this historical analysis a better-informed understanding of the present role of the state in the industry, its rationale and its effect. More specifically, the book will examine what effect IT policy is having on the conditions and prospects for the industry to develop in a sustainable manner.
- Third to outline a broader research agenda on the industry with the intention of promoting a more effective form of state intervention. More specifically, the book will identify the key constraints and opportunities facing the industry and discuss the important policy issues they raise.

1.3   STRUCTURE

The book is structured and presented in three parts.

Part 1 comprises Chapters 2, 3 and 4. It provides a background and context to the study.

Chapter 2 provides an overview of the global software services industry. The widespread public acceptance of the politically motivated literature on the Indian software industry stems in part from a general lack of comprehension of what exactly the global software services industry is. The chapter addresses this by outlining the three-tier structure of the industry, introducing its major firms and charting the evolution of the industry. It is intended that by providing such information, the reader will be better able to understand how the Indian software services industry developed within the wider framework of the Indian and global IT industries (as presented in Part 2).

Chapter 3 critically reviews the most influential arguments purporting to explain the industry's phenomenal growth in India. These are: technological advances in telecommunications allowed India to plug itself directly into the global software services industry; Indians have a particular intellectual proclivity for software programming; the implementation of neo-liberal policies in India freed entrepreneurial spirits and allowed the country to exploit its comparative advantage; and the inspired interventions of a 'developmental department' fostered the industry. The intention of the chapter is twofold: first, to show why all of the above are, at best, only partial explanations; and second, to highlight how the flawed state-versus-market approach prevalent in studies of development has distorted an understanding of the industry's transformation.

Chapter 4 presents an alternative analytical framework to understanding development. Taking as point of departure the problems inherent in the state-versus-market approach, the framework adopted in the book stresses the need to make concrete connections between economic interests, the interventionist policies implemented and the structural transformation of the industry engendered. The intention of the chapter is to familiarise the reader with the framework adopted in the book, as well as to highlight its superior analytical features.

Part 2 comprises Chapters 5, 6, 7 and 8. It examines the development of the IT industry in India from 1970 to 2010, with special reference to the software services industry.

Chapter 5 presents the period between 1970 and 1978. This was the first phase of the industry's development. The chapter explains how and why the state played a leading role in establishing a national Indian IT industry via the establishment of Indian computer production and the promotion of software exports. It highlights how the demonisation of this period by neo-liberals is by no means justified: while the policy was far from flawless, significant achievements were made during this period.

Chapter 6 examines the period between 1978 and 1986. This was the second phase of the industry's development, initiated after the election of the Janata Party to political power in the late 1970s. The chapter describes how the IT policy regime ushered in by the new Janata government was designed to favour a narrow set of commercial interests via instigating changes in the computer hardware industry. However, while this spelt disaster for the technological capabilities of the Indian computer industry, it inadvertently catalysed the growth of Indian software firms.

Chapter 7 describes the period between 1986 and 2000. This was the third phase of the industry's development. The chapter describes the interventions by the Indian state in the software industry during this period, highlighting how they chimed with the state's larger economic concerns. During this period the largest Indian software firms began to capture major segments of the software services market in the West, and with it, the world's attention.

Chapter 8 details the development of the industry over the past decade, 2000–10. This is the fourth and final phase of the Indian software industry examined, and is characterised by the rapid influx of IT-related FDI and major volatility in the Indian labour market for software programmers. The chapter explains how and why Indian software services firms, which started the new century with prospects for rapid development, have started to experience major problems in upgrading or expanding towards the latter part of the decade.

Part 3 comprises Chapters 9 and 10. Taking the findings from Part 2 as point of departure, it presents the implications and wider lessons derived from the development of the IT industry in India.

Chapter 9 concerns itself with the implications of the findings for the future trajectory of the industry itself. The chapter paints a depressing portrait of the industry, highlighting how it is rapidly being transformed from a potential global frontrunner in software services into a low-value-added back office of the world. It also explains why the state is uninterested in the industry's deteriorating situation, unabashedly continuing with an IT policy which is exacerbating the conditions leading to retrogression. It concludes with an outline of a research agenda which could help to reshape IT policy.

Chapter 10 discusses the wider lessons derived from the pattern of development undergone by the Indian software services industry. The chapter begins by refuting the conventional policy wisdom (promoted relentlessly by the World Bank) that developing nations can, and should, emulate the Indian software services industry by implementing tax breaks and subsidies to attract IT-related FDI. It then moves on to argue that the development of the industry forces a reconsideration of the role of the Indian state in development. Finally the chapter ends by identifying the negative consequences attached to the widening political influence of NASSCOM.

The book's closing chapter summarises the findings and locates the Indian IT industry as presented in Parts 1–3 in the wider economic, social and political milieu of the nation.

Part 1
The Context

2
The Global Software Services Industry: An Overview

You have fibre-optic lines running parallel with bullock carts ... the US doesn't understand [the Indian software industry]. The world doesn't understand [the Indian software industry].

Chief executive officer (CEO) of an Indian software firm[1]

2.1 INTRODUCTION

The CEO quoted above could not have put it better. The reality of the Indian software industry, captured perfectly by the hallucinogenic image of optic fibres and bullock carts, continues to bedevil most people. While much of the misunderstanding can be attributed to politically motivated distortions (see Chapter 3), a lack of understanding with regard to the global software services industry per se has also played a part. This chapter endeavours to pave the way for a clearer understanding of the Indian software industry's growth by providing a brief overview of the global software services industry, presenting a succinct account of the structures, firms and processes of this much misunderstood sector.

2.2 BENEATH THE TIP OF THE IT ICEBERG: THE SIZE AND STRUCTURE OF THE HIDDEN INDUSTRY

Few people outside the IT industry are familiar with the software services industry. In contrast, everyone in the developed and developing world is familiar with the software package industry (also referred to as the software product industry). Indeed, the software package industry's most high-profile son, Bill Gates, is reported to be one of the most famous people in the world. In contrast, few people outside of the corporate world have even heard of Cap Gemini, a software services behemoth with annual revenues close to $10 billion. Odd then that the software services industry is of roughly equal size to the software package industry.[2] And its

9

biggest firm, IBM, has far larger revenues than the leading software package firm, Microsoft.

The reason for the software services industry's low profile is its character. The global IT Industry is like an iceberg – only its tip is visible, comprising the high-profile industries of computer manufacturing and software packages. Most of the industry, however, exists beneath the surface, none more so than the software services industry, often referred to as the hidden industry.

Software services firms usually provide highly specialised software services – such as systems integration, custom applications and IT consulting – to corporate or governmental clients.[3] Unlike software packages, software services are, in effect, hidden, embedded in IT systems beyond the purview of individual users.[4] For example, when using a major metropolitan underground transport network, one is not even aware of the IT system responsible for running it smoothly, let alone the huge investments, financially and in intellectual manpower, required to create, maintain and upgrade such systems. The only persons therefore fully au fait with these firms are those that work in them and those IT managers in corporations and governments who are responsible for contracting out software services to them.

Due to the diversity of the software services required by different corporations and governments, the structure of the industry is highly stratified. As evidenced by Figure 2.1, there are three key tiers. The lowest tier comprises IT outsourcing in the form of basic data processing and maintenance. In this book Business Process Outsourcing (BPO), such as the third party provision of front-desk operations (e.g. call centres) and back-office operations (e.g. payroll management), is also included in the IT outsourcing tier. As would be expected, there are low barriers to entry in this tier. Price is of prime importance when IT managers decide who to contract such services to and firms with the lowest prices tend to win the contracts.

The middle tier involves higher-level services in the form of writing customised software applications which enable a firm to carry out highly individualised tasks particular to that client organisation. Such applications are often referred to as enterprise software. Here a software services firm's track record and reputation is of importance in winning contracts, bringing with it certain barriers to entry. It is possible for a firm which has at first provided IT outsourcing services to a corporation to subsequently move up to writing enterprise software.

The top tier of the software services industry involves IT consultancy. This requires responsibility for the design and construction of an entire IT project from start to finish. Here, experience of similar projects is crucial, as is reputation: the barriers to entry are high. Such contracts are usually awarded to a small, select group of firms. Firms involved in IT consultancy are also usually engaged in business consultancy more broadly defined.

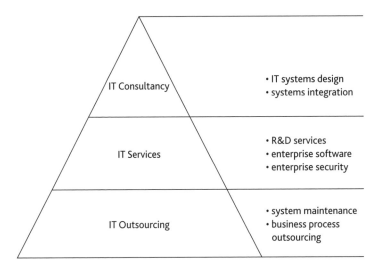

Figure 2.1   The Three-Tier Structure of the Software Services Industry

2.3   THE MAGNIFICENT SEVEN: INTRODUCING THE GLOBAL GIANTS AND THE INDIAN MAJORS

The firms in the software services industry vary greatly in size and capabilities. Of importance to this book are the Global Giants and the Indian Majors.

2.3.1   The Global Giants

Four firms dominate IT consultancy: IBM, Accenture, EDS and Cap Gemini. They are often referred to as the 'Global Giants' or 'Giants' for short. As the term 'Global Giant' indicates, they are all very large and also very global. All firms have high-end IT consulting capabilities but also offer various other services. Of the four, IBM is by far the largest, dwarfing the other three firms. For example, IBM's total revenues are nearly $100 billion and it employs nearly 500,000 people. In contrast, both EDS and Accenture have revenues closer to $20 billion and employ roughly 150,000 people. Cap Gemini has revenues of approximately $10 billion and has a workforce of just over 120,000. Moreover, the firms have very different histories and, while all four overlap in IT consultancy, they also operate in different sectors.

IBM has the longest history per se, and is also the most embedded in the IT industry. Many still perceive IBM as a computer hardware manufacturing company. However, by the mid-1990s IBM had already started a major corporate restructuring process, shifting its core focus from computer manufacturing to software services. In 2002 it acquired PwC Consulting to further its consultancy capabilities. But the seismic shift was finally completed in 2005 with the sale of its computer manufacturing line to the Chinese firm Lenovo.

EDS also has pedigree in the IT industry. However, unlike IBM, EDS was never a computer manufacturer. It was established in 1962 as a data processing firm but quickly developed into a leading software services firm with higher-end capabilities. In 2008 it was acquired by the computer manufacturing behemoth HP and renamed HP Enterprise Services. Like IBM a decade earlier, it is likely that HP will increasingly focus on software services and HP Enterprise Services will become the central division within the firm.

Cap Gemini was founded in 1967, over half a decade after IBM. It is a French company and began in data processing and enterprise management. Through mergers and acquisitions as well as organic development, it quickly developed global prominence in higher-end software services. Paralleling IBM's purchase of PwC Consulting, Cap Gemini strengthened its business consultancy capabilities by acquiring Ernst and Young Consulting in 2002.

Accenture started as a small data processing division within Arthur Anderson, the global accountancy group. However, in line with the general trend towards outsourcing of software services in corporate America in the 1980s, the data processing division expanded rapidly within the larger accountancy firm, Arthur Anderson. In 2000, it split from Arthur Anderson and changed its name to Accenture.[5]

As noted, the Global Giants do not solely provide IT consultancy. Rather, they are all involved in what can be divided into two distinct types of service. First, they provide software services across all tiers of the industry. Second, they provide business services, which essentially means management consultancy. IBM and EDS arguably have the greatest strengths in software services, while Cap Gemini and Accenture are more formidable in management consultancy.

2.3.2 The Indian Majors

There are three Indian Majors: Tata Consultancy Services (TCS), Infosys and Wipro. These firms are far larger than any of their other compatriot firms. Like the Giants, the Majors have varied histories. TCS began in 1968 as part of the Tata conglomerate. In contrast, Wipro's first foray into the IT industry was in computer manufacture in 1980, with software services a sideline (see Chapter 6). It was only in the late 1980s that software services began to become the firm's core focus. Infosys was established in 1981 as a breakaway from another Indian IT firm. It has always been a software services firm.

However, despite their different histories, over the past two decades they have converged in terms of the services they offer, their size and their capabilities (and shortcomings). Of the three, TCS is the largest. But only marginally so. Its revenues are just over $8 billion and its workforce numbers approximately 200,000. Infosys and Wipro are of similar size, each with revenues approaching $7 billion and workforces close to 150,000.

Their structural development has also been in tandem from the late 1980s onwards. For example, once telecommunications infrastructure was provided, all began providing lower-end software services to the US market by remote delivery (see Chapter 7). This helped the Majors move up the value-chain throughout the 1990s and early years of the twenty-first century. In addition, all have struggled in terms of breaking into the highest echelons of software services, IT consultancy (see Chapter 8). Figures 2.2 and 2.3 provide an indication of the differences in revenues and employment between the Giants and the Majors.

2.4 CREATIVE DESTRUCTION AND THE DEVELOPMENT OF THE INDUSTRY, 1950–85

The software services industry has gone through a number of profound changes over the past 40 years. These changes have been overwhelmingly determined by the character of the installed computer hardware base to which software services firms have access. In other words, the development of the software services industry is subordinate to, and shaped by, technological and commercial changes in the computer manufacturing industry. This section will explain the industry's development up to the mid 1980s.

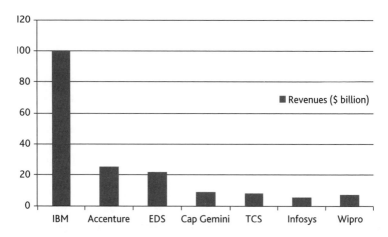

Figure 2.2   The Giants and Majors by Revenue Stream

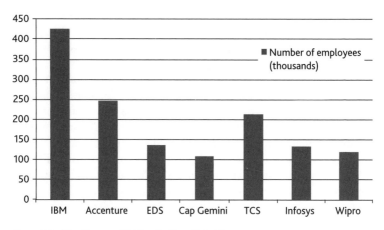

Figure 2.3   The Giants and Majors by Size of Workforce

The software services industry originates in the 1950s and 1960s when computers began to be adopted by governments and large corporations. However, the market for specialist software services firms in the 1950s was small as it was customary for computer firms to write software for their computers and sell the hardware with the software already attached (a process known as bundling). And specialist software would tend to be written in-house by the corporation or government buying the computer. As such, the software services firms that did exist grew slowly during this period.

The first fillip to the industry occurred in the 1960s, following the decision to unbundle software and hardware by the dominant computer manufacturer IBM.[6] This, in theory, allowed software services firms to write specialist software for the purchasers of IBM computers. The market for IT services thus expanded. At the same time, other firms were entering the industry from a slightly different angle. These firms provided basic data-processing services to corporations. And hence the IT outsourcing tier of the industry was born.

The next boost to the software services industry came in the late 1970s when the computer hardware industry was revolutionised by the microchip in what has been referred to as the PC (personal computer) revolution. The advances in price/performance of semiconductors alongside the standardisation of computers led to the production of small, inexpensive yet relatively powerful computers – the PC. Suddenly, computers were not just lumbering, exorbitantly priced mainframes. The widespread uptake of PCs by corporate America massively expanded the software services market in the USA across all three tiers, particularly IT consultancy (see Chapter 7).

2.5   CONVERGENCE AND CATCH-UP IN THE INDUSTRY, 1985–2010

The first important trend has been the growth of remote delivery of software services from the late 1980s onwards. Prior to that, IT services were delivered onsite at the client's headquarters in a process known as body-shopping. And while firms specialising in IT outsourcing were not exactly required to be located next to the client, proximity was important.[7] However, as a result of rapid advances in telecommunication technology, ever more data could be transmitted at ever lower prices and with ever increasing reliability. This meant, in theory, IT services and IT outsourcing could be delivered from anywhere in the world to anywhere else in the world. And yet, due to the highly idiosyncratic manner in which the IT industry had developed in India, the only firms in the developing world able to exploit this new found opportunity fully were Indian (see Chapter 7). Thus, Indian software services firms were at the forefront of this new mode of software services provision and had a virtual monopoly on such provision throughout the 1990s.[8]

A second trend has been the evolution of the integrated services model from the late-1990s onwards, whereby software services firms provided services across tiers, from highest-end IT consulting to low-end IT outsourcing. The integrated services model was pioneered by the most successful Indian software firms – the Majors – who capitalised on their rapid growth via remote delivery of IT outsourcing and basic IT services to diversify up the value chain into higher-end software services. This was primarily via the acquisition of small Western business and/or technology consulting firms. Given the intra-firm efficiencies generated by the provision of integrated services, it was soon copied by the Global Giants. Their method of emulation was primarily by acquisition. However, reflecting the different tier being entered, the targets of the Giants' acquisition strategy were Indian firms providing BPO services to Western firms by remote delivery.[9]

A third trend was the development of the global delivery model, whereby software services firms provide integrated services from centres all over the world. Initially, this was a consequence of the manner in which the Majors and Giants achieved their integrated services model. Via acquiring firms in different segments of the software services industry (IT consultancy firms in the West, BPO firms in India) a global delivery model for the provision of services developed passively. Majors provided much of their higher-end services through their IT consultancy acquisitions in the West, while the Giants delivered their lower-end IT services and IT sourcing through their acquisitions in India. However, since 2005 both Giants and Majors have scaled up their presence in India and the West through organic growth, representing the extension of the global delivery model independent of the integrated services model. The Majors have even started to establish delivery centres in other parts of the developing world (see Chapter 9). The scale of global operations can be best captured by the firms' employment statistics. For the Giants, approximately one in three of their employees is based in India. For the Majors, approximately one in five of their employees is based outside of India, primarily in the West.

The result of all three trends has been that the Majors and Giants increasingly resemble each other in services provided, manner in which they are delivered and locations from where they are produced. An industry-defining contest is in full-flow between the Giants, who wish to preserve their dominant position in higher-end software services, and the Majors, eager to break into the select club.

2.6   CONCLUSIONS

This chapter has attempted to present an outline of the global software services industry. It first described the industry in terms of its current size and structure. It then presented an overview of the key firms in the industry. The chapter concluded by describing the evolution of the industry over the past half-century, paying particular attention to trends over the previous two decades. It is intended that this information will help pave the way for a clearer understanding of the development of the Indian software services industry presented in Part 2 of the book.

3
The Development of the Software Industry in India: Existing Explanations and their Shortcomings

For the IMF and its supporters, India is a case study proving economic reform works. It has brought faster growth, particularly in those parts of the country and of the economy that have opened up most to competition and have been least shackled by government. The most obvious example is the IT industry.

The Economist[1]

The fact that conceptions about reality, and ideologies and theories, are influenced by the interests as commonly perceived by the dominant groups in the society where they are formed, and that they so come to deviate from truth in a direction opportune to these interests, is easily seen and, in fact, taken for granted when we look back at an earlier period in history.

Gunnar Myrdal[2]

3.1   INTRODUCTION

The juxtaposition of a high-tech, transnational, dynamic industry emerging in a country which has generally been seen as a byword for backwardness, isolation and stagnation is inevitably going to draw global attention. And so, over the past decade, academic, governmental and media literature on the Indian software services industry, the largest and most competitive in Asia, has proliferated. Journalists, scholars and policymakers have all sought to interpret the phenomenon, producing a cornucopia of explanations for the presence of an advanced software services industry in India but not elsewhere in the developing world.[3] This chapter reviews the main arguments and propositions.

3.2   TECHNOLOGICAL ADVANCES

Thomas Friedman, the New York Times columnist, Pulitzer Prize-winning author and arch guru of globalisation, has been amongst the most prominent of the industry's observers. Upon surveying the Bangalorean landscape, where bullock carts roam between imposing glass and steel skyscrapers housing the world's top software firms, Friedman memorably pondered in the opening pages of his bestselling book on globalisation, *The World Is Flat*, whether this juxtaposition of ancient and modern was 'the New World, the Old World, or the Next World'.[4] Given the book title, Friedman rather predictably concluded that the Indian software industry was a manifestation of the emerging 'flat world' in which geographical distance was being rendered ever more irrelevant by advances in telecommunications, allowing people and nations to compete on a more equal footing than at any previous time in the history of the world.[5]

There is of course an element of truth in this: advances in telecommunications have been a key driver of the provision of services by remote delivery, of which India has been the principal beneficiary.[6] But Friedman is disappointingly light on why India, and not China or Brazil, should have been at the forefront of such a style of delivery. English-language proficiency is unimportant – software services, except for front-desk operations, require only basic syntax and a limited vocabulary – and cannot therefore be considered an adequate explanation.[7] Friedman is also unable to explain why certain Indian software firms should be able so dramatically to out-compete, not only in scale of software services provision but also in technical capabilities, firms from all other countries bar the USA and Germany.[8] His trim offering of 'good timing, hard work, talent and luck' cannot be considered an adequate explanation.[9]

3.3   INTELLECTUAL APTITUDE

A popular explanation for the Indian success has been the notion that Indians have a particular aptitude for software programming. What Friedman alludes to as 'talent', Cheryll Barron expands on in an article for the journal *Prospect*. Barron proposes a causal link between the Sanskritised culture of Indian antiquity and contemporary India's pre-eminence in software.[10] She argues that the Indian education system places a greater emphasis on abstract thought processes than other systems, which, she claims, is a result of the enduring influence of ancient Sanskritised learning methods. As these abstract thought processes are highly conducive to software programming, Indians have an intellectual comparative advantage in the sector.[11]

The aptitude thesis put forward by Barron faces a major problem in that the link between the Indian education system and software aptitude is not at all clear. The Indian education system, in which learning by rote, a product of colonial-era educational thinking rather than Indic antiquity, is central to the curriculum, has been widely criticised for suppressing, rather than enhancing, abstract thought. Tellingly, NASSCOM has been amongst the most vociferous critics of Indian education, arguing that it stifles creativity. Despairing at the rote-learning system, the association has actually promoted a restructuring of the Indian education system to make it more 'IT-friendly'.[12] Therefore the education system in India as it currently stands, whatever its ancestry, cannot be deemed a primary explanatory factor in the growth of the country's software industry.

But what of an innate aptitude amongst Indians for software programming independent of the education system?[13] This has been contemptuously dismissed by one scholar as an attempt to 'draw a straight line from the Vedas to the Silicon Valley'.[14] However, rather than an appealing *ex post facto* explanation for the development of the software industry, the view of a natural talent amongst Indians served to bolster government support for the software industry before it blossomed. For example, TCS's first managing director, F.C. Kohli, often referred to as the father of the Indian software industry, made such a claim in 1975 while addressing the Computer Society of India:

Many years ago, there was an industrial revolution. We missed it due to factors which we had no control over. Today, there is a new revolution – a revolution in Information Technology – which requires neither mechanical bias nor mechanical temperament. *Primarily, it requires the capability to think clearly. This we have in abundance.* We have an opportunity even to assume leadership. If we miss this opportunity, those who follow us will not forgive us for our tardiness and negligence [my emphasis].[15]

'Vijay', a contributor to one of *Business Week*'s many blogs, puts forward a similar view of an intellectual comparative advantage in rather starker terms. 'Americans can't compete with my Indian brothers and sisters', he claims, before going on to dismiss the former as 'stupid'.[16] Even American firms seem to have bought into the hype: a minor brouhaha erupted in 2005 when a New Jersey-based software company advertised *explicitly* for Indian software programmers.[17]

But should you believe the hype? There are definite links between a logical mind, an aptitude in mathematics (according to Albert Einstein, 'pure mathematics is the poetry of logical ideas'), and the ability to write software. This is undisputed. But are Indians really better at mathematics and, therefore, at software programming?[18] Given the problems with international comparisons, those claiming that Indians have a special aptitude for mathematics and software programming tend to focus on the educational performance of Indian students in multi-ethnic societies. In both the USA and the UK Indians do tend to perform the best in educational attainment across all ethnic groups (including white Americans and British), and this is particularly pronounced in mathematics and the sciences.[19] This has been verified by every possible disinterested source.

Taking such facts at face value, there might seem to be a case. However, a number of other issues need to be considered. To understand better the performance of students of Indian origin in the USA and the UK, it is necessary to consider other factors such as social class (Indians tend to be the most professionalised of all ethnic groups in both countries, with implications for educational attainment), family background (due to immigration policies, Indians in the West tend to come from scientific and technical backgrounds, influencing the subject preferences of their children) and perceptions of the job market (views of endemic racism in the labour market, particularly in the UK, has meant Indians have tended to expend more effort in education generally, and in subjects with greater employability, such as mathematics in particular).

Thus, the notion of some genetic or racial link between Indians and software programming must be tempered by a whole array of social factors. Moreover, even if an innate ability can be demonstrated, it cannot alone explain the growth of the software services industry in India. After all, logical thinking and mathematical ability are integral to various others industries which have not, as yet, developed in India.

3.4   NEO-LIBERALISM

There are two different neo-liberal interpretations of the rise of the Indian software industry. The first claims that the 1991 economic liberalisation provided the necessary conditions for the Indian software services industry to emerge. The second view acknowledges that the industry experienced rapid growth prior to 1991, but claims that this was due to its evasion of the Indian state's interventions; in the words of one neo-liberal scholar, 'it flew under the radar'.[20]

The first interpretation perceives a sequential relationship between the 1991 liberalisation and the rapid growth of the industry. It is accompanied by either explicit assertion or underlying assumption of cause and effect: that economic liberalisation led directly to the Indian software industry as we now know it. Most such works take 1991 as an analytical starting point, presuming no Indian software industry existed prior to the 1990s. Even when the presence of a software industry in India in the 1970s and 1980s is acknowledged, attention is focused on its negligible revenues during this period – a fact used as evidence for the argument that the regulationist framework of the era had failed by comparison with what was to come.[21]

However, a cursory glance at the pre-1991 literature and data on the Indian software industry demonstrate just how empirically dubious is the above interpretation. While it was only in the 1990s that significant revenues began to be generated by the industry, the compound annual growth rates (CAGR) for software exports from India in the 1970s was approximately 50 per cent, rising to 58 per cent in the 1980s. In comparison, between 1998 and 2008 the CAGR of software exports from India was only 27 per cent.[22] Therefore there is no empirical evidence to support the argument that the 1991 liberalisation sparked the rapid growth, let alone the emergence, of the Indian software industry.

The second neo-liberal interpretation acknowledges the rapid growth of the Indian software industry prior to 1991. However, it claims it was the industry's fortuitous evasion of the distorting effects of state intervention during the period of dirigisme that allowed it to grow organically. This evasion, it has been argued, was due to the state's lack of interest in the software industry vis-à-vis manufacturing and heavy industries. A group of US and Indian economists sarcastically declared that the Indian government 'actively encouraged' the growth of the industry by 'choosing not to interfere much in the process of industrial development'.[23] V.N. Balasubramanyam refers to the role of the state as one of 'benign neglect'.[24]

While more accurate in its chronological understanding of the industry's development than the other neo-liberal interpretation, the notion that the industry 'flew under the radar' of a disinterested state still runs into empirical problems. For example, as long ago as the 1960s software was first mooted as a potential export industry for India. Moreover, and in atypical haste, the Indian state acted on this conjecture: by 1972 it had implemented the Software Export Scheme; and by 1974 the first exports from India took place. Furthermore, the scheme's premise – the tying of domestic support to export performance – has continued to be the modus operandi of the software industry in India.

3.5   THE DEVELOPMENTAL DEPARTMENT

The 'developmental department' literature (DDL) is based on the Developmental State Paradigm, which attributed East Asia's rapid development after the Second World War to effective, market-distorting state intervention. The paradigm argues that such state interventions in East Asia were more effective than elsewhere in the developing world due to the region's specific socio-political conditions. These conditions, particularly the authoritarian character of the governments, allowed East Asian states to exert an autonomy over policy that was beyond the means of other states in the developing world.[25]

Reflecting its intellectual heritage, the DDL claims that the Indian state was able to intervene more effectively in the Indian IT industry than in other industries because IT policy was in the hands of an autonomous and developmentalist department: the Department of Electronics (DoE), much feted by the Indian media and Western academics alike. Other departments and ministries of the Indian government were, by contrast, deemed to be permeated with vested interests, busily subverting policy and thereby impeding development.[26]

In essence, the DDL has reconciled the requirement for state autonomy with India's vibrant democracy and influential special interests by presenting the DoE as an autonomous institutional actor within the Indian political economy.[27] The turn in the DoE's IT policy in the late 1970s, away from state control and towards greater private-sector involvement, is attributed to a new breed of bureaucrats in the DoE. This view is best expressed by Professor Balaji Parthasarathy, who claims that 'policy changes' were due to 'a few reform-minded bureaucrats'.[28] Professors Murali Patibandla and Bent Pederson are even more effusive about the DoE personnel from the late 1970s onwards, referring to them as 'dynamic local technocrat–entrepreneurs'.[29]

By acknowledging the integral role of the Indian state's interventions in the development of the Indian software industry, the

DDL is on a much firmer empirical footing than earlier neo-liberal interpretations. Nonetheless, the literature suffers from three major deficiencies.

First, due to its intellectual lineage, it assumes that providing evidence of autonomy is sufficient to explain the industry's development. As such, the focus of the DDL was in justifying an autonomous DoE rather than explaining how the industry had developed: the industry's underlying structural transformation has received far less attention in the literature than justifying the autonomy of, and then detailing the changes of personnel in, the DoE.

Second, the case for autonomy over IT policy relies on extremely flimsy evidence. The DoE's alleged autonomy rests on the assumption that software firms in the 1980s were small and therefore lacked sufficient power to influence the state. But this overlooks the impressive organisation, mobilisation and cohesion of the Indian software services firms at the time.[30] It also ignores the presence of other interests with a stake in IT policy, such as India's Business Houses, computer hardware manufacturers and global capital, which certainly did have the capabilities to influence government.[31]

Third, by adhering to the theoretical requirement of autonomy, the literature avoided contrarian evidence documenting in detail the subversion of IT policy by vested interests.[32] For example, Chapter 6 illustrates that it is far more likely that the personnel changes within the DoE in the late 1970s were made at the behest of vested interests, to get rid of bureaucrats committed to dirigisme and replace them with 'yes men', rather than being the result of a random but massively significant introduction of 'technocrat–entrepreneurs'.

The Developmental Department literature is, therefore, far from convincing.

3.6 CONCLUSIONS

The achievements of the Indian software services industry have bamboozled most people around the world. This is partly because India was, until the industry started to develop, not seen as being particularly sophisticated in technological or commercial terms. The confusion also lies in the fact that major economic powers have also failed to make much headway in developing an indigenous, internationally competitive software industry. The United Kingdom has ceased to be a 'viable, independent IT base'.[33] Similarly, the software industry in Japan 'remains in its infancy'.[34] This chapter has discussed the four major schools of thought purporting to explain the success of the Indian software services industry.

The technological and aptitude explanations for the development of the Indian software were shown to be severely limited. While entertaining and populist, neither school provided much more than tenuous links or anecdotal evidence to verify their respective claims. The neo-liberal and DDL interpretations both focused on the role of the state and were more substantive. Neo-liberals perceived the industry's growth as being the outcome of India's comparative advantage, realised through the absence of state intervention. In contrast, the DDL has proclaimed the presence of a 'developmental department' as the root cause of the industry's spectacular growth. But despite their contrasting viewpoints, both neo-liberals and adherents of the DDL offer similar and deficient analytical approaches, which serve only to obfuscate the actual pattern of the industry's development and the role and rationale of state intervention in shaping it.

First, both literatures overwhelmingly focus on either the market or the state as mechanisms in bringing forth development. In the neo-liberal literature, liberalisation policies are alone deemed a sufficient explanation for subsequent development; and policies which are not market-friendly are completely ignored. Similarly, the DDL is guilty in the main of merely reeling off state policies, assuming that the intended objectives within policy documents come to fruition. It even feeds into the neo-liberal literature somewhat by drawing attention to the positive impact of the DoE's liberalisation agenda. For example, according to one of the DDL's biggest advocates, former DoE Secretary N. Vittal, 'the Indian software export miracle happened because something ungovern-ment-like happened: the DoE started breaking rules to create a freer environment, which dramatically changed the scenario'.[35] As a result of their shared deficiencies, both literatures are peppered with unsubstantiated linkages between policies and industrial outcomes based on stylised facts and figures. Moreover, the fixation on state and market has meant a lack of attention on *why* specific policies have been adopted at certain times.

Second, and related to the above, in both sets of the literature the theoretical or ideological tail has been guilty of wagging the empirical dog. For advocates of the 'developmental department', the 'tail' has been the need to demonstrate autonomy and assume all policies as technocratic and developmental, at least once rapid growth had started to take place. Unfortunately, this has led scholars to exercise a degree of selectivity, actively or subconsciously, over what evidence to include, what to rework in line with established assumptions, and what to overlook. Selectivity towards the evidence base also applies to those presenting a neo-liberal interpretation, not least in that they overlook evidence of the industry's growth prior to 1991 and the positive impact of certain state interventions.

Third, as a result of theoretical and ideological point scoring, little attention has been given to the underlying economic relations across the IT industry and how the various interventions have impacted upon them. The lack of attention paid to the substantial linkages between software and computer hardware industries in India, despite their mutual dependence being common knowledge, has been particularly damaging in understanding the evolution of the Indian software services industry. Just as such linkages have played an integral role in affecting the pattern of development in the IT industries of Japan and Taiwan,[36] computer hardware policies in India have been integral to the development of the local software industry.[37]

To conclude, both sets of literature are guilty of casually quoting facts which support their wider claims and omitting or reworking, subliminally or deliberately, facts which are less corroborative. In part, this stems from the ideological and theoretical biases of the scholars or commentators concerned. But it also reflects their shared approach: the academically dominant but analytically limited state-versus-market approach, which privileges state and market over societal forces and industrial conditions in interpreting the processes of development. The result has been a superficial understanding of the forces that have driven and are driving IT policy in India as well as the structural transformations the industry has undergone and is undergoing. The following chapter will illustrates how such flaws can be addressed via the construction of an alternative and superior analytical framework.

4
The Political Economy Approach to State Intervention and Industrial Transformation: An Analytical Framework

The history of all hitherto existing society is the history of class struggles.

Karl Marx[1]

4.1 INTRODUCTION

Academic confusion over the industry's development is a result of an inability and reluctance to comprehend the dynamic relationship between the state's interventions and the industry's structural transformation. The dominant neo-liberal narrative claimed the absence of state intervention had propelled the industry to its remarkable success, despite overwhelming evidence of the active role of the state. The 'developmental department' literature (DDL), despite acknowledging the role of state intervention in the industry's development, failed to grasp the rationale behind such interventions. Relatedly, it misinterpreted many of the industrial outcomes such intervention engendered. The purpose of this chapter is to construct a superior framework by which to analyse the industry's development, taking as point of departure the problems inherent in the DDL.

4.2 THE WHO AND WHY OF POLICY: THE INTERESTS BEHIND STATE INTERVENTION

The DDL has been marked by the absence of works that have gone beyond the DoE in trying to understand why distinct IT policy agendas were pursued at different times. For example, Peter Evans ascribes the shift from state control to state regulation of the IT industry as a result of a change in the leadership of the DoE, from bureaucrats inclined towards a more statist approach to those with a more market-friendly attitude.[2] There is no wider analysis of why this change in leadership was taking place or how it may or may not have tied in with the wider concomitant shifts in Indian political economy.[3] This narrow focus is a result of the literature's analytical starting point of state autonomy, which assumes that outside forces played no role in IT policy formation.[4]

In contrast, the approach taken here not only rejects the Developmental State Paradigm's notion that autonomy is a prerequisite for effective state intervention, but also claims that it is not even an attainable reality.[5] The state's interventions in the IT industry, regardless of whether it engendered developmental outcomes or not, will instead be understood as reflecting the interests of, and power configurations between, dominant economic interests. The 'why' of interventions in the IT industry will be located within the societal milieu in which it is deemed to have been formed rather than referred back to an apparently technocratic government department.

There are five key steps to developing an understanding of state intervention based on the above premise. These are listed below.

- The first step is to understand how society (including class and fractions of capital) and state interact in the formulation of interventionist policy. To do this it is necessary to privilege class and fractions of capital over the state; that is, first to identify class and fractional interests and then examine if and how they manifest themselves in the state. The state should be perceived not as independent of society but as reflective of society; a terrain of conflict, contestation, negotiation and compromise between different, often antagonistic, interests.

- The second step is to comprehend the diversity of interests within an industry. On the rare occasions when such interests are acknowledged, they have tended to be presented as monolithic. However, there is no uniform interest. For example, local computer hardware firms and local software firms have evolved with very different, often conflictual, interests. Moreover, the interests of domestic software capital and those of foreign capital within the software services industry in India have become increasingly antagonistic of late.[6] The various interests should be accepted and understood, not brushed aside and forgotten.

- The third step is to understand the scope of analysis. Even when analyses have acknowledged the role of commercial interests in policy formation, they have tended to examine only those interests immediately associated with the industry. Thus, for an excellent political economy analysis of the South Korean car industry, the economist Kwon-Hee Lee examined just three economic interests: domestic car assemblers, component makers, and foreign car makers.[7] Such limited scope is, however, not viable in examining the Indian IT industry. Given the importance of access to computers for large-scale organisations, the Business Houses have always had an interest in IT policy in India. Moreover, following the recent trend in the establishment of 'captives' in India providing in-house ITES for their parent firm, foreign capital, from British Airways (with its call centres in Hyderabad) to Nokia (with its software development centre in New Delhi) has become increasingly interested in the character of that country's IT policy. Thus, analysis must be both international and multi-sectoral.

- The fourth step is in understanding how interventionist policy is forged amidst the variety of interests with different, often competing, motives. A nuanced understanding of the interactions between such interests is integral to this. It is not a case of the more or most powerful interests imposing the policy that best serves their needs. Often a policy agenda serving the dominant economic interests can be blocked or diluted by a coalition of interests that would lose out from such a policy. Therefore the eventual intervention should be perceived as a compromise, based on negotiation and cooperation, as well as conflict, among and between economic interests and political decision makers.

- The fifth and final step is accepting that the economic interests attached to an industry are not fixed but are constantly evolving in line with changing global, national and sectoral conditions at political, technical and economic levels. In short, they are always in a state of flux. After all, by structurally transforming the industry, state intervention will inevitably create new winners and losers. While the immediate winners may be easily identified, given the complexity of the IT industry and the shifting dynamics of global accumulation, the dominant economic interests that emerge over medium to long term may well be different. The fundamental point is that any meaningful analysis must be sensitive to the evolution of such interests and avoid complacency in ascribing what they might be.

4.3   THE EFFECT OF POLICY: A STRUCTURAL ANALYSIS

Both the neo-liberal literature and the DDL rely excessively on the Compound Annual Growth Rate (CAGR) of the industry's revenues and exports as evidence of development. It was customary in the DDL to attribute an increase in CAGR to the most recent policy implemented. For the neo-liberal literature it would be traced back to the most recent liberalisation measure. The CAGR fixation has produced three major deficiencies in analysing and understanding the industry's transformation.

First, it led to the inflation of the developmental effects of certain policies and, concomitant with this, the 'developmental' abilities of the DoE. Production and export figures are prone to fluctuations independent of policy shifts. For example, much of the growth of the Indian software industry has been made possible by the phenomenal growth of the global market for software alongside advances in telecommunications technology, both of which have been independent of Indian IT policy. CAGR is far more likely to reach double digits for an industry when the global market for its products and services is expanding at similar rates than if the global market were stagnant.[8] Acknowledgement of this should dampen, or at least qualify, the praise meted out to the DoE. In other words, Professor Vibha Pingle's assertion of the vast superiority of the Department of Electronics over the Department of Steel in India, based on the superior CAGR of the software industry, should be tempered by acknowledging that the global market for software services grew far more rapidly than that for steel.[9]

Second, it led to certain policies being assigned a 'developmental' role when they in fact played a minimal role in the industry's development. For example, the Software Export Policy was singled out as being crucially important to the subsequent growth of the Indian software industry.[10] The logic is clear if flawed: the software industry during the early 1980s began to grow rapidly and as the only policy document at the time discussing software was in 1981 (the aforementioned Software Export Policy), it was deemed that the two must be causally related: the policy led to the growth. However, it was a negligible policy, concerned with changing the minutiae of state policy towards the software industry. It had little effect on the growth in the software industry at the time. The growth was driven by changes in the installed computer hardware base brought about by a policy shift with regard to the computer hardware industry. It had nothing to do with any software-related policy. In the development of the Indian software industry, contrary to the account given by the DDL, the Software Export Policy should be no more than a footnote.

Third, the lack of industrial knowledge has allowed certain anti-developmental policies to be categorised as developmental. For example, a certain IT policy has been described by one scholar as inducing 'impressive achievements'[11] while another scholar claimed that, as a result of the same policy, 'the computer industry, in terms of production and technology, began to take off'.[12] Both scholars were impressed with the seemingly great strides made in the production of computers following the implementation of the policy.[13] However, upon closer inspection, there was no 'production' taking place. The policy being venerated did not boost genuine production, but ushered in an illicit trading regime in which 'knock-down' computer kits (i.e. kits containing the parts needed to build a computer – essentially computers in 'flat-pack' form) were imported from East Asia and merely assembled in India in makeshift factories.[14] A reliance on production figures had led to a fundamental misunderstanding of the outcomes from a major IT policy.

In order to understand better the software industry's transformation, and in particular the role of policy in engendering it, a structural rather than growth-centred analysis needs to be applied. In other words, the structure of the Indian IT industry as a whole needs to be taken as the analytical starting point for any investigation into the development of the Indian software industry. This structure is underpinned by three major economic relations, as illustrated in Figure 4.1. The most important relation is that between local software capital and the domestic computer hardware manufacturers (and installed base). The second significant relation exists between each fraction's connections with foreign capital. The third relation is the competitive structure of the hardware industry.

Therefore, from the point of view of understanding an industry's pattern of development, the only policies that matter are those that restructure the industry; those, that is, that change one or more of the industry's economic relations (it is often the case that a policy to directly restructure one of the relations has a knock-on effect on the other relations). Such policies can be considered truly transformative. Policies that do not meet the criterion of restructuring one or more of the industry's economic relations, regardless of whether they receive more attention or require greater financial outlays than transformative policies, are of substantially

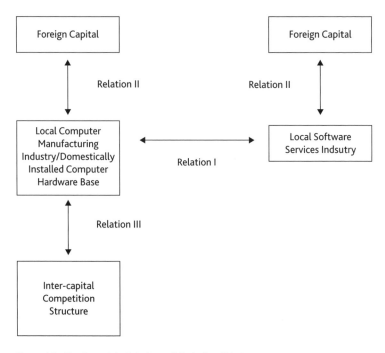

Figure 4.1   The Economic Relations of the Indian IT Industry

less importance. They merely facilitate or retard the existing system of accumulation attached to the industry's structure.

4.4   CONCLUSIONS

As evidenced, existing literature on the development of the Indian software industry has failed to identify the interests behind IT policy in India. It has also struggled to grasp the complicated manner in which policy has influenced the Indian software industry's pattern of development. This chapter has introduced the methods by which the interests behind policy can be better identified and the ways in which the effects of policy on the industry's transformation can be more accurately evaluated. These insights are applied to the development of the industry in Part 2 of this book.

Part 2

The Development of the Indian IT Industry

5
IT Started with a War: The Establishment of the Indian IT Industry, 1970–78

I mean, what does India export but communicable disease?
Daniel Patrick Moynihan, Ambassador to India (1973–75)[1]

5.1 INTRODUCTION

How did the Indian IT industry begin? It has come to be believed that the answer lies in the liberalisation of the Indian economy in 1991 and the commercial dynamism it unleashed. This view is simply wrong. Any meaningful analysis of the Indian IT industry as it is now must begin with an examination of the early 1970s. In this period an active, interventionist IT policy was first constructed and then rigorously enforced. These interventions, while far from flawless, succeeded in establishing a national computer firm and, unbeknown to Ambassador Moynihan, software exports. This chapter will explain how and why.

5.2 THE WIDER CONTEXT: THE STATE OF INDEPENDENCE

5.2.1 Of Guns and Butter: The End of Subordination to Indirect Western Control

There is a widespread assumption that India became independent in 1947. In one sense, this is correct: political sovereignty *was* handed over to Indians in August 1947. However, the capability of the Indian government to implement domestic policies according to its own will and needs was heavily circumscribed. Despite the formal transfer of power, Western powers retained considerable control over Indian domestic policy. In the words of the historian R. Palme-Dutt, Indian independence in 1947, despite both fanfare and bloodshed, was merely a transition from direct British rule to indirect Western rule.[2] Understanding how indirect Western rule was maintained and why it came to an end is a significant element of understanding the how and why of the state's interventions in the IT industry in the 1970s.

Indirect control was enforced by a variety of levers which would be applied should the Indian government ever stray out of line. The most important of these levers was access to food.[3] At independence, India was barely able to feed itself.[4] Maintaining access to food imports was thus a high priority for the Indian government, particularly in times of drought. A bad monsoon would, therefore, necessitate a massive importation of food which, given India's financial constraints, could only be met on concessional terms. Invariably, the only country able to offer concessions on such a scale was the USA, leading to Indian dependency on US largesse. This situation famously ensured India's compliance with the US operations in Vietnam.[5] More importantly, it meant that India would not be able to follow policies which went against US interests until it achieved food self-sufficiency.

The other key Western lever over the Indian government was Pakistan. Pakistan is considered by many scholars of South Asia to be the creation of Western and, in particular, British political scheming and geopolitical strategising in light of decolonisation and the emerging Cold War. In the opening pages of *The Shadow of the Great Game* (2007) Narendra Singh Sarila, a former aide-de-camp to Lord Mountbatten, the last British Viceroy of India, writes:

Once the British realised that the Indian nationalists who would rule India after its independence would deny them military cooperation under a British Commonwealth defence umbrella, they settled for those willing to do so by using religion for the purpose. Their problem could be solved if Mohammed Ali Jinnah, the leader of the Muslim League Party, would succeed in his plan to detach the northwest of India abutting Iran, Afghanistan and Sinkiang and establish a separate state there – Pakistan.[6]

While Pakistan was primarily established as a base and bastion for the projection of Anglo-American power into the Middle East and South-East Asia, its proximity to India also served to inhibit the Indian government from pursuing policies which might be deemed negative in London and Washington.

Owing to these conditions, the Indian government's economic policies following independence were highly conservative, particularly with regard to how Western capital was treated.

However, one outcome from development policy and one war changed the power relations between India and the West.

First, as a result of development policy in agriculture, by the late 1960s India had become much less reliant on food imports. Post-independence investments in irrigation, subsidies on fertilisers, and changes in the land tenure system had started to pay off. Agricultural yields began to improve significantly, which in turn led to a reduction in India's importation of food grains. For example, in 1966 India had imported 10.34 million tons of food grains. By 1968, food grain imports had halved to 5.69 million tons. And by 1971 they had fallen to 2.03 million tons.[7] This situation, bolstered by better food distribution networks, meant that droughts could be addressed domestically. The Indian government no longer needed to rely on the US government (and acquiescence to the conditions attached) to prevent a drought from turning into a famine.

Second, by the end of 1971 India's preoccupation with a perceived Western military threat, articulated via Pakistan, had faded. The 1971 Indo-Pakistani war, in which, with Indian military support, East Pakistan had broken away and formed Bangladesh, had significantly weakened the Western proxy, Pakistan. Not only had the split halved Pakistan's economy and population, it had removed from Pakistan its most fertile and resource-rich region. From a more direct national security point of view, India no longer had to consider hostile Pakistani forces along thousands of miles of its Eastern borders. Perhaps the most important fallout was the Pakistani military's loss of confidence and acceptance of inferiority. Professor Stephen Cohen of Harvard University, writing after the Indo-Pakistani war of 1971, regarded India's 'preeminence over its neighbours as so substantial that its position [as regional hegemon] has been recognised by all major outside powers, and implicitly so by all South Asian states as well, even including Pakistan'.[8] The Treaty of Peace, Friendship and Cooperation with the USSR, signed during the build-up to the war, merely added to the Indian government's new found sense of security from potential Western aggression.

In short, both proverbial guns and butter had together released the Indian state from subordination to Western rule by rendering the levers of such indirect control irrelevant. As a result, from the early 1970s onwards Western capital in India could no longer be assured of freedom of operations.

5.2.2   The Business Houses Fall from Favour

Kafka and Swift, as much as Marx and Hobbes, serve as astute guides to domestic Indian political economy. Class interests and power relations regularly manifest themselves in surreal, Kafkaesque regulations worthy of mockery and satire. One of the oddest individual alliances of all was the close relationship Mahatma Gandhi, paragon of modest living and promoter of cottage industries, had developed with India's richest industrial oligarchs.[9] By the time of independence, Gandhi had taken this affinity to a whole new level, seeing out his final months in the palatial home of G.D. Birla, India's wealthiest businessman. However, Gandhi's relationship was merely the most extreme manifestation of a much wider political paradox in India at the time of independence: the close personal and financial ties between the avowedly socialist leaders of Indian independence and India's largest conglomerates, referred to as the Business Houses.

How can we understand this? While contemporaneous works on India generally caricature the Nehruvian era as socialistic, a better word would be corporatist.[10] Via close personal connections, as well as through generous donations to the freedom movement, the Business Houses were able to exert huge influence on the newly established Indian government's agenda. The state was to protect and nurture the Business Houses, not displace them. Moreover, foreign imports of capital goods (including computers) were to be allowed until adequate (cheaper and of near equal quality) replacements were available domestically. Under no circumstances would the Business Houses be in favour of any attempt to foreclose the ability to import a capital good unless adequate domestic alternatives were in place.[11] Given their interests and influence, the Business Houses enjoyed a veto over the state's industrial policies.

This domestic situation reinforced the Indian state's conservatism imposed by indirect Western rule. However, just as the West's leverage over the Indian state began to erode by the 1970s, so too did the Business Houses' domestic influence over the government. The how and why is integral to understanding the formation of IT policy at the time.

The roots of this erosion lie in the changing fortunes of the Congress Party. Up to the 1960s, the Congress Party *was* the party of government. All other parties paled into insignificance in terms of nationwide reputation and inter-class support. However, throughout the 1960s support for Congress dwindled. This was partly a result of the death of Prime Minister Jawaharlal Nehru, the Party's talisman and symbol of independence. It was also an outcome of the Party's inability to translate its lofty socialist rhetoric into substantial improvements in the living standards of the common man. To stop the slide further, Congress needed to find new ways to win votes.

To this end, they began to court a group in society referred to subsequently as the intermediate class, the petty producers of rural and small-town India.[12] Their high status and central position in rural backwaters and small urban towns gave this class an impressive ability to mobilise votes for Congress. In return for ensuring strong voter turnout for Congress, the intermediate class sought, amongst other sops, to extend the number of manufacturing sectors reserved exclusively for SMEs.[13] This was, however, directly in conflict with the Business Houses' desire to see such reservations dismantled.

As political imperatives increasingly forced Congress to extend reservations for small-scale production in return for the political support of the intermediate class, the Business Houses lost faith in Congress and in particular Prime Minister Indira Gandhi. They began to look elsewhere. They switched their allegiance (and financial backing) to the pro-business political party, Swatantra. Moreover, they started to encourage the anti-Indira faction within Congress, known as the Syndicate, to usurp power. Both strategies, however, spectacularly backfired. In 1969, in a bid to starve Congress's political party rivals of funds (a move directed in particular against the Business House support for Swatantra), Indira Gandhi banned political donations from companies. And in the early 1970s, in a feat of political manoeuvring worthy of praise from Machiavelli himself, Indira Gandhi emasculated the Syndicate and in particular its leader, Moraji Desai.[14]

As a result, by the early 1970s the Business Houses had lost their privileged connections to the government of India. They were now outsiders, *personae non gratae* in the corridors of power in New Delhi. More importantly for the IT industry, their de facto veto over industrial policies had been revoked.

5.3   INTERESTS AND INTERVENTIONS: THE BOMBAY IT PARTY

Yet by the early 1960s elements within the Indian state had started to take an interest in an active, interventionist IT policy.[15]

The Sino-Indian conflict in 1962 had brought home to the Indian defence establishment the importance of technology for national security.[16] A vital factor in India's defeat in that conflict had been the superior information technology at the disposal of the Chinese armed forces. Access to modern computer technology, as well as supporting electronics, now came to be perceived as vital for defence purposes. The arms embargo imposed by the USA on India following the Indo-Pakistani war of 1965 also emphasised the need for an indigenous production base for advanced electronics, including computers. The interests pushing for an indigenous computer capability were centred in the Department for Atomic Energy, headquartered in Bombay (now Mumbai).

Other elements of the state saw IT through the developmental prism. Professor Narasimhan, a prominent Indian scientist, had identified the software industry as a sector of enormous export potential for a country like India. Writing in a 1968 Government of India Report *Computers in India*, he explains his reasoning:

> [Software] is a labour intensive activity except that it requires intellectually skilled manpower ... Software development would seem to have a very high employment potential in a country like India ... the export potential, as well as the value added, in the case of software is very large.[17]

There was also interest in Indian IT policy from the private sector, both foreign and Indian. However, the interest was in blocking, rather than promoting any IT policy and, in essence, in preserving the status quo. For transnational computer corporations (TNCCs) such as IBM, this meant resisting the state's attempts to regulate and control their trade and production activities further. For the Business Houses, it meant the state's non-interference in their computer procurement practices. As they purchased their computers from the TNCCs, and relied on the same firms for service and maintenance of their computers, their interests were tied in with the interests of the TNCCs.

For most of the 1960s, the status quo was preserved. This reflected the wider context of the decade. The political dominance of Business Houses domestically, combined with the vulnerability of India to Western leverage, meant that the urges to develop a domestic IT industry – which might have encroached on TNCCs' freedom of operation and the Business Houses' unimpeded procurement – were suppressed. However, by the early 1970s the Business Houses' influence had been frittered away and any vestiges of Western leverage over India had ceased. This new-found context massively empowered the elements within the state apparatus – centred in and around the Department of Atomic Energy in Bombay – pushing for a more interventionist IT policy.

By mid 1970 the state had established a government department with the sole remit of formulating an interventionist IT policy: the Department of Electronics (DoE). The DoE's three initial policies, adopted soon after its establishment, would significantly transform the Indian IT industry.

The first of these was the launching of a national champion in computer manufacture, Electronics Corporation of India Limited (ECIL). The domestic manufacture of computers would ensure that embargos would not undermine India's computer capabilities. It was decided that ECIL would be the beneficiary of what is often referred to as 'infant-industry protection'.[18] The firm would be protected from external and domestic competition via trade protection and domestic monopoly on production respectively (the domestic monopoly would be applied to the higher-end class of computers). Protection from competitors would help the firm to achieve economies of scale. In addition, it would allow it to concentrate on mastering technical learning rather than more commercial imperatives. It was also expected that the domestic monopoly would ensure that resources which were scarce in India – highly skilled labour, capital and technology – would be most effectively utilised in a single computer firm rather than spread thinly across many competing firms. Moreover, ECIL would benefit from a special status in government procurement practices as well as government subsidies.

The attempt to bring TNCCs present in the Indian IT industry (particularly IBM) under Indian control through dilution of their ownership was the DoE's second and far more controversial policy. Neo-liberal literature on this policy has demonised this move, describing it as 'draconian'. What is less often noted is that the move to dilute ownership was in step with wider government policy to control the activities of TNCs in India (embodied in the 1973 Foreign Exchange Regulation Act – FERA for short) and had a developmental rationale. According to numerous government reports and academic studies in the 1960s and early 1970s, TNC operations in India (including those of IBM), rather than bringing in technology and foreign exchange, led to a net outflow of foreign exchange and other deleterious effects on the economy. With Western leverage over India a thing of the past, the Indian state in the early 1970s now felt that it was finally possible to address this issue and exert pressure on TNCs to align their operations more closely with the Indian state's developmental strategies. Dilution was considered one tool by which the Indian state could achieve such alignment.

The rationale behind the move was certainly applicable to IBM. Of the various TNCs operating in India, IBM was singled out in more than one report as the biggest offender. Its 'abuse' of a bureaucratic loophole had allowed it to exert a stranglehold on the market while importing outdated, second-hand and overpriced computers for resale in India.[19] Moreover, its operations were seen as leading to a net export of foreign exchange. Dilution of the IBM subsidiary as a means of obtaining control over its activities was therefore most apposite. Control would not only curb many of IBM's economically damaging activities, it would also facilitate the country's computerisation as well as support a more favourable balance of payments.

In the event, IBM refused to dilute its stake in its subsidiary. The IBM president, John Maisonrouge, speaking in 1973 at the United Nations in New York, outlined the rationale behind the firm's policy of maintaining 100 per cent control of all its subsidiaries. He argued that as 'every IBM computer system is designed by several laboratories around the world and manufactured in several plants, trying to fit this kind of product into subsidiaries with shared ownership raises all kinds of management-control problems'.[20] In short, he was claiming that the transnational nature of IBM meant shared ownership was simply not a viable option.[21] Instead of dilution, IBM made a number of alternative offers – including a high export commitment from domestic production. These offers were all turned down by the Indian government.[22] IBM – at the time the largest corporation in the world – was forced to close down its Indian operations in 1977.

However, the absence of IBM in the Indian market prompted another computer firm – Britain's International Computers Limited (ICL) – to engage in a joint venture.[23] ICL deemed the potential commercial gain through enhanced market share as outweighing any costs attached to sharing managerial control. The dilution strategy was therefore a mixed blessing: while the dilution of IBM failed, the TNCC behemoth's departure initiated a smaller TNCC's agreeing to dilution.

The DoE's final intervention was reliant on neither the emasculation of Business House influence nor the decline of Western leverage. Rather, it was an appendage to the first intervention; a supporting act to the main attraction of developing a national champion in computers. In view of the costs attached to developing a national champion in computer manufacture, the DoE sought ways to generate foreign exchange in order to justify these financial outlays. Software exports, drawing on Narasimhan's report years earlier, was perceived as the most appropriate method of reaping foreign exchange. As Joseph Grieco, an early observer of the industry, has written:

> [I]t was the foreign exchange earned [by software exports] that the Commission and Department [of Electronics] pointed to when it needed to justify its requests to the Planning Commission and Finance Ministry to support ECIL's computer effort.[24]

And so the 1972 Software Export Scheme was born. The scheme set out to harness the software programming talent within India's management consultancies. While providing software services was by no means the chief source of income for these consultancies, they would often have on their books a number of people educated in computer software and would lease them out to Business Houses to write specific software programs. This process – an early, domestic form of body-shopping – was widespread enough to have come to the attention of the bureaucrats working within the DoE.

The scheme sought to transform these management consultancies with a side interest in software services provision into bona fide software firms competing in the global market. How would it do this? First, it needed to get firms to sign up to the scheme. It did this by providing 100 per cent loans on computer purchases to all firms that signed up. Given the small size of such firms and the prohibitive costs of computers at the time, this was the only means by which firms could gain access to their own computers. It was, therefore, a significant incentive. Second, it needed to ensure that firms would use these computers to produce software for export rather than for the domestic market. As such, firms signing up to the scheme were prohibited from providing services to the domestically installed hardware base. Moreover, loans had to be repaid through foreign exchange generated only via the export of software. Far from failing, within two years the scheme had established an export-oriented software services industry in India.

5.4   WHAT HAPPENED? INDIAN COMPUTERS AND SOFTWARE EXPORTS

It is no surprise that the three policies outlined above had a significant effect on the character of IT in India. How could they have failed to do so? This section examines how the interventions affected the underlying economic relations of the industry.

5.4.1   Relations Between the Local Computer Industry and Foreign Capital

The development of ECIL as a national champion in computer production established a computer manufacturing industry in India. Prior to this there had been no such industry – India had relied on importing computers from US corporations. This situation was disadvantageous for a number of reasons: it made India vulnerable to embargoes; it blocked access to the most advanced computers as the imports were also already outdated; and it impeded computerisation as the imports were often overpriced (in 1970 there were just over 100 computers in the whole of India).[25] It was expected that the establishment of ECIL would address all these issues.

These expectations were partially met. By successfully achieving indigenous computer manufacturing capabilities, ECIL reduced India's vulnerability to embargoes. Moreover, by the mid 1970s ECIL had started to produce relatively advanced computers. While somewhat short of the technological frontier, the computers in the TDC series were merely a few years behind the world's most advanced computers. From a purely technological point of view, the strides taken were impressive.

What let ECIL down was its failure to achieve anything approaching mass production. As early as 1975 there was a growing feeling within the DoE that ECIL's production would not be capable of meeting India's computer requirements.[26] ECIL's failure in mass production was a result of its own success in establishing a genuinely indigenous, relatively advanced computer manufacturing capability. A fixation in the early years on developing a comprehensive understanding of base knowledge in computer production had delayed production.[27] Subsequently, an off-limits approach to purchasing foreign technology had led to the firm focusing more on mastering technical learning than on engendering economies of scale.

The dilution of ICL was less successful. Joseph Grieco was the most enthusiastic commentator about the outcomes from the dilution. He wrote that following its dilution, ICL had started 'undertaking activities which complemented and supported the government strategy to foster a more independent computer industry'.[28] ICL definitely gave assurances of increasing assembly of computers in India as well as some export commitments.[29] However, according to a DoE bureaucrat at the time, the diluted company continued to serve as an export outlet for its parent company, going so far as to refuse to develop local manufacturing linkages.[30]

5.4.2   The Relations of the Local Software Services Industry

The 1972 Software Export Scheme was the most successful of the state's three policy interventions: it succeeded in creating an export-led software industry in India decades before most countries would even consider the possibility. Tata Consultancy Services (TCS) was the first firm to join the scheme. It had been established in 1968 and its first software services project was to write the software programmes for the Central Bank of India. Within two years of signing up to the scheme, it was exporting software to corporations in the USA.[31] There is little doubt that its parent company Tata was important in securing such contracts, in particular by utilising its emerging commercial relationship with the US computer firm Burroughs.[32]

TCS's success in exports had two effects which spurred the growth of the export-oriented software services industry in India. First, it proved the feasibility of the export model (albeit with a major body-shopping component) to firms contemplating joining the scheme. Thus, once TCS's exports took off, many firms rushed into the scheme. This is shown by the fact that only 35 computers were imported under the scheme between 1972 and 1975 and yet, between 1976 and 1981, an astonishing 441 computers were imported.[33] Second, TCS provided evidence to sceptical Western corporations that Indian firms were able to deliver quality software services. This was important since in the 1970s India was more renowned for leprosy than for customised software, as reflected in Ambassador Moynihan's derogatory remark quoted at the beginning of the chapter. An excerpt from a case study on TCS by the Indian Council for Market Research highlights this path-breaking role:

> By consistently undertaking and performing good quality jobs for clients at a fraction of the cost they would otherwise have incurred, TCS put India on the global map and became a premier IT outsourcing destination for companies in the West, particularly the US. Crediting TCS with bringing glory to the Indian IT industry, Nandan Nilekani, CEO of TCS' competitor, Infosys Technologies, said, 'TCS pioneered the Indian software industry and has played a seminal role in the global acceptance of the Indian software capabilities'.[34]

However, despite the scheme's achievements, it also suffered from a number of deficiencies.

Preventing firms from engaging in any form of domestic software provision was the major flaw in the scheme. Domestic software services provision could have acted as a springboard to export success, allowing firms to build up technical and commercial capabilities in the domestic market for subsequent application in the more competitive export markets. TCS had won its first international contract on the back of the software services it had provided in the domestic market in the late 1960s (that is, prior to the scheme being established).[35] By foreclosing such an avenue for firms entering the industry (and the scheme) in the mid 1970s, most of the software firms found themselves in a low-value-added, body-shopping relationship with their overseas clients, and with limited scope for migration up the value chain.

Another serious flaw stemmed from the DoE's under-appreciation of the logistical problems involved in exporting software. For example, much of the services provision would take place at the client's headquarters. While in a domestic situation this would have limited negative effects, leasing out programmers to clients in the West entailed all sorts of logistical headaches regarding visas, travel and accommodation. In addition, the costs attached to the body-shopping process would significantly lower profit margins. The DoE could have ameliorated such issues by providing subsidies for travel and accommodation, providing help with visas and even setting up flats in major US metropoles to be used by Indian software firms' programmers. But it did not.

Alongside the two aforementioned issues, there were also problems with meeting prospective overseas clients. While TCS could rely on parent company Tata both for direct contact and reputation (important in securing a contract in IT services), other Indian software firms did not enjoy such advantages. They would have to rely on their own marketing campaigns. But a major complaint by software firms during the 1970s was that foreign exchange for such marketing events was extremely difficult to obtain.[36] The DoE could have made such funds available and promoted overseas marketing campaigns itself, as it did in the late 1980s and throughout the 1990s.

The above deficiencies in the scheme can best be understood by the context in which the DoE conceived it. As previously stated, the DoE saw software exports as a foreign exchange generator necessary to justify the ECIL effort. As such, they sought to generate as much foreign exchange as possible within a couple of years. The easiest way to do this was to foreclose all domestic service provision even if such provision would facilitate technical learning and higher export revenues over the longer term. The prioritisation of computer hardware manufacture over software export also explains the lack of logistical support afforded to software exporting firms. The software firms were simply expected to get on with their job of generating foreign exchange and to resolve their own problems. The eyes of the DoE were firmly fixed on the computer hardware industry.

5.5 CONCLUSIONS

In recent years many scholars have characterised this period in the Indian IT industry as one of unmitigated failure. Policies have been labelled as misguided, bureaucrats caricatured as ideological and impractical, and industrial development as laggard. In reality, the outcomes of the DoE's initial interventions were far less clear-cut. Yes, an export-led software industry had failed to grow at the rates

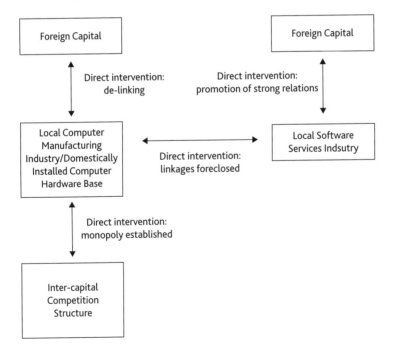

Figure 5.1   Relations at the End of 1977

many expected. However, Indian software firms had still managed to establish commercial relations, albeit fragile and dependent, with a number of foreign clients during this period.[37] More importantly, they had done so far earlier than the software firms of most other countries, an advantage which will become clearer in subsequent chapters. In addition, a genuinely indigenous computer hardware industry had been established in India. This was no mean feat. And, after initial teething problems, by the end of 1977 ECIL had doubled its computer production from that of the previous year.[38] By the late 1970s the system of accumulation in the Indian IT industry – as illustrated by Figure 5.1 – appeared highly conducive to rapid growth. However, as the following chapter illustrates, this would soon be disrupted.

6
Catalytic Corruption: The Domestic Software Services Boom, 1978–86

The law of unintended consequences illuminates the perverse unanticipated effects of legislation and regulation.

Robert Norton[1]

6.1   INTRODUCTION

Given the Indian software industry's holier-than-thou image, corruption is not a word one readily associates with it. Yet it has played a major role in the industry's development. This chapter explains how corruption and the law of unintended consequences combined to produce an unprecedented boom in the market for software services in India, catalysing its growth between 1978 and 1986.

6.2   THE WIDER CONTEXT: BACK TO BUSINESS – THE EMERGENCY AND THE RETURN OF THE OLD GUARD

India is credited with being a vibrant, long-standing, stable democracy. This is only partially true. While other countries surrounding it succumbed to numerous coups and slipped into dictatorships of various hues, India did remain committed to parliamentary democracy – except, that is, between 1975 and 1977. On 26 June 1975 India 'transformed from being a working democracy to a personal dictatorship'.[2] In more detail, parliament was dissolved; freedom of speech criminalised; unions and strikes banned; and habeas corpus suspended. This period, referred to in India as the Emergency, has been widely forgotten in the West. And yet, though it lasted for less than two years, it set in motion a complete transformation of the domestic political economy, with implications for all industries, including IT.

6.2.1   Business and Politics During the Emergency

By the end of the Emergency, the Business Houses were firmly back in the corridors of power in New Delhi. The roots of this rapprochement lay in the pattern of accumulation initiated during the period 1975 to 1977. While explanations for the Emergency differ – with the government claiming it was a response to national security threats and opponents claiming it had much more to do with Indira Gandhi's own thirst for power – all are agreed it had nothing to do with the Business Houses. However, while the Emergency was called for reasons unrelated to the Business Houses, by outlawing strikes and imprisoning the most militant trade unionists the biggest beneficiaries were the large industrial conglomerates: with no days lost to strikes, industrial production boomed; and with wages frozen, profits soared.[3]

Flush with cash and aware that the Emergency would be a temporary phenomenon and elections would be called sooner or later, the Business Houses set about insuring themselves with any future government. They did this in the time-honoured fashion of pumping huge amounts of money into both major political parties (Congress and Janata), wisely hedging their bets. And both parties, despite their 'socialist' credentials, gladly accepted the funds. Congress knew that in order to have any chance of re-election, they would require a substantial war chest; and, well aware that only the Business Houses were able to finance such a campaign, they were only too keen on courting them.[4] The Janata Party, an ad hoc coalition of parties united only in their opposition to the Emergency, also gladly accepted Business House funding, recognising that without such cash supplies victory could not be assured.[5] Big business and politics, estranged for a decade, had once again become entwined in India's political economy.[6]

6.2.2   Business and Politics after the Emergency

By the time of the election in March 1977, the Business Houses were in a supreme position. As a result of the political economy that had emerged during the Emergency, they had been able to translate their economic wealth into political capital. Unlike the political parties contesting the election, the Business Houses could not lose: no matter which way the majority of people voted, their interests would be safeguarded. After a break of nearly a decade, the election would herald a return of the Business Houses to the policymaking process.

This was, of course, masked by the political rhetoric. Both main political parties contesting the election – Congress and the Janata – espoused socialism and economic nationalism. Their speeches paid homage to the plight of the peasant, the cancer of corruption, and the injustices of inequality. They also stressed the importance of self-reliance in technology.[7] The only economic division to speak of between the parties was related to certain aspects of 'socialism'. Janata's emphasis on the need to decentralise the economy stood in contrast to the more state-centric views of Congress.[8]

In the event, the Janata Party won the election. Its period of rule embodied the sharp contradictions between the political rhetoric of small-scale socialism and the political reality of Business House influence. For example, on coming to power the party proclaimed that it was 'dedicated to the task of building up a democratic, secular and socialist state in India on Gandhian principles drawing inspiration from our rich heritage and the noble traditions of our struggle for national independence and individual liberty'. And yet it took no time in selecting as prime minister a close friend of the Business Houses and avowed anti-socialist, Moraji Desai. One would be hard-pressed to find a person who was less likely to convert India into a bona fide socialist state.[9] However, while the selection of Desai spoke volumes about where the new locus of power lay, other actions were far more veiled and deceitful.[10] This would be reflected nowhere more so than in IT policy – a masterclass in grand deception.

6.3   INTERESTS AND INTERVENTIONS: ILLUSIONS OF GRANDEUR

There were three direct interests in Indian IT policy at the end of the Emergency: the Business Houses; the DoE, specifically those involved with ECIL; and the wider public, particularly the higher echelons of the scientific community and sections of the political elite.

The Business Houses were keen on removing barriers to their procurement of computers from abroad. They had never been sold on the idea of a national champion in computer manufacturing, perceiving it as an impediment to their plans for expansion and profit maximisation. However, their own estrangement from political influence by the early 1970s had severely constrained their ability to challenge that policy forcibly. All they could do was to articulate a number of attacks via the media on the protection afforded to ECIL. That global computer prices had fallen dramatically since the early 1970s while ECIL's computers had remained expensive further exacerbated the Business Houses' anger with existing IT policy. Now, with 'their man' Moraji Desai as prime minister, they began pushing for change.

The interests of the Business Houses, however, came into conflict with those of the DoE. The DoE had focused much time and effort on developing ECIL's computer manufacturing capabilities. And, while manufacturing capabilities had progressed slowly, the firm had gained a solid foundation in technological capabilities. Furthermore, over recent years, manufacturing capabilities had improved massively. For the DoE, any decision to end ECIL's protection would be counterproductive; it would undermine the technological and manufacturing advances painfully forged over the preceding eight years. It might even signal the death knell of ECIL. As such, the DoE was fiercely resistant to any change in IT policy.

The Indian people, in particular its scientific and political elites, also had an interest in IT policy. Computers were a prestige industry, and the ability to manufacture them was considered by some as tantamount to development. Economic and technological nationalism was embedded more firmly than ever in Indian culture and any moves perceived to be undermining domestic computer manufacturing capabilities would be heavily opposed by influential forces within Indian society.

This, therefore, placed pressure on the Janata Party. It had stressed economic nationalism and technological self-sufficiency in its election manifesto and was painfully aware that any policy shifts to the contrary would be seized upon by the opposition as evidence of anti-national sentiments; a 'told you so' by Congress to the general public.[11] At the same time Janata's backers, the Business Houses, were demanding an end to current IT policy and immediate access to cheaper computers. How could the state reconcile these interests?

There were two options to resolve the situation. One was to consider how best to foster a more productive indigenous computer manufacturing industry. This would involve bringing together the various interests to consider policy changes and seek compromise over a new policy agenda that would be acceptable to all. The other was to draw up a policy which would appear outwardly to address the needs of all interests but implement it in a manner which would pander to the most directly powerful interest – the Business Houses. The first option would involve a great deal of effort, cajoling and time. Moreover, there was no definite prospect of success. The second option would merely require policy manipulation, good public relations and large-scale deception.

The easier, second option was selected by Janata: the interests of the Business Houses would be addressed as much as possible, while the other interests would be deceived or eliminated. Machiavellian scheming rather than Weberian administration would inform the character of the intervention.[12]

The first priority was to change the DoE's top brass before any substantive policy shift could take place. Those with a genuine commitment to self-sufficiency in computer production, and also honesty and integrity, were a real threat and obstacle. They had to be removed so that policy shifts would be smoothly complied with and whistle-blowing prevented. The most senior victim of the cull was the DoE's secretary, Professor M.G.K. Menon. He was a firm believer in self-sufficiency and closely connected with ECIL and the Department of Atomic Energy.[13] His colleague, mentor and close friend had been Homi Bhabha, one of the strongest advocates of Indian technological self-sufficiency and the inspiration behind many of the DoE's early policies.[14] If Menon remained in charge of the DoE, he could be expected to mount a serious challenge to any policy shifts that might undermine ECIL or self-sufficiency. He was transferred almost immediately after the Janata victory to the Department of the Environment, Science and Technology.

Yes-men with no links to ECIL or the atomic energy community were swiftly brought in to replace him. Menon's direct successor as DoE secretary was Professor B. Nag. He was a complete outsider who, according to Professor Balaji Parasarathy, 'had no links with the atomic energy network' and was 'not committed to the idea of self-reliance and protecting ECIL'.[15] Moreover, to distance ECIL from the Department of Atomic Energy and the rest of the Bombay IT party, ECIL also had a new managing director in the person of S.R. Viajayakar. According to Parasarathy again, this was a man with a 'pragmatic approach to the question of foreign technology and self-reliance', in other words another outsider.[16] Such an attitude appears to have served him well – in 1984 Viajayakar took over from Nag to become the DoE's third secretary.

With the 'troublemakers' out of the loop and yes-men in, the next step was to sell a new policy to the public which would tick nationalist and developmentalist boxes while also providing scope for the Business Houses to meet their computer requirements. And so the Minicomputer Policy was born.

The buzzword in the policy report was competition. ECIL's poor production figures were blamed on a lack of competition rather than on issues of technical learning. Therefore, it was argued, the introduction of competition into the sector would be the panacea to production difficulties: the introduction of private-sector firms would lead to a rapid leap in computer production, a substantial drop in prices and, soon enough, a computer-laden country. The report assured readers that firms entering the computer industry would be strictly vetted by a licensing system. Firms would, first and foremost, have to be Indian: no technical or financial collaboration with foreign firms or governments was to be allowed. Moreover, it claimed that the licensing system would be strictly enforced, engendering controlled competition and thereby producing the necessary market conditions for the licensed computer manufacturing firms to expand rapidly and achieve economies of scale. It also stated that domestic production of components and peripherals would be prioritised in order to develop a local IT complex and prevent foreign-exchange leakage.[17] And finally, it declared that ECIL would remain protected in the higher-end computer market. The report therefore ticked all the necessary boxes.

The only thing left for the Janata Party and their yes-men in the DoE to do was to 'implement' the policy so that the Business Houses could meet their computer requirements quickly and effectively. To achieve this, the actual interventions were very different in practice from what they were on paper. The implementation would be carried out so as to ensure that computers would be immediately and widely available in India. Three policy features stand out in achieving this goal. They are:

- First, in the first two years over 40 licences for computer production were issued; and by the end of 1981, 86 applications for licenses had been approved. With so many licences and entrants, it would be difficult for firms to develop viable production volumes over the long-term. But, by providing computer manufacturing licences to any firm that wanted one, the bureaucrats of the DoE did ensure that the maximum number of computers became available in the immediate term.
- Second, the DoE had made no attempt to establish a local peripherals and components industry which could supply the computer hardware firms. Most of the firms therefore operated what could be considered a screwdriver assembly system: importing knock-down kits and simply putting them together.

The DoE looked the other way when these kits were imported. Allowing the importation of such kits not only ensured that computers were available immediately, it also created what was, in effect, a veiled retail outlet for foreign computer firms.

- Third, the DoE equally turned a blind eye to the importation of higher-end computers which encroached on ECIL's monopoly in that area.[18] This broke with the commitments in the Minicomputer Policy and ensured that ECIL could never be a national champion in computer manufacture. It did however allow the Business Houses, the only organisations that would need and could afford high-end computers, access to the cheapest available.

Moreover, just to underline how uninterested the DoE was in fostering a viable computer hardware industry in India and, instead, how determined it was to give Business Houses unlimited access to imported computers, it started to renege on its earlier responsibilities.[19] When the ICL joint venture started to return to being an export outlet for its British parent company – which directly contravened its commitments – the DoE did absolutely nothing to stop it.[20] Indeed, one could argue that it encouraged such behaviour.

While this may look like a developmental disaster, from the viewpoint of the Business Houses and the DoE it was a huge success. The policy's intention was, after all, to create a system which, on paper, looked indigenous but was, in reality, a veiled computer-import system. The industry-level implications of such a short-termist, narrow policy agenda will be discussed in the following section.

6.4   WHAT HAPPENED? A POSITIVE CASE OF UNINTENDED CONSEQUENCES

Far from being a period epitomised by the dynamic development of the domestic computer hardware industry, as some observers have claimed, the years following the end of the Emergency witnessed the industry's destruction and replacement by an import system by stealth. However, like a phoenix from the flames, out of the smouldering ashes of the national computer industry sprang forth a rapidly growing software services industry. By examining the effects of the Minicomputer Policy on the underlying economic relations of the industry, this section explains why and how.

6.4.1 The Competition Structure of the Indian Computer Manufacturing Industry

The licensing system engendered by the Minicomputer Policy was the major policy shift and is therefore the key starting point in any analysis of industrial outcomes. Far from a selective and discriminatory procedure, the DoE was essentially offering licences to any Indian firm applying to enter the computer hardware industry. Within the first three years this had translated into over 80 licences being issued. In contrast, the Japanese state had issued just six firms licences for computer production a few years earlier.[21]

This impacted directly, rapidly and negatively on the competitive structure of the Indian computer hardware industry. The outcome was a heavily fragmented industry comprising numerous small computer firms. Lumbered with limited market share, excessive price competition and uneconomic scale, most firms were unable to generate the profits required for reinvestment in upgrading and expansion. Even the larger domestic firms, such as HCL, Sterling and Wipro, with the potential to be national champions, did not reinvest their profits into expansion and upgrading, preferring instead to encash them.[22] Reinvesting profits with a longer-term view of breaking into export markets made little sense in the absence of government commitment towards developing the industry.[23]

6.4.2 Relations Between the Local Computer Manufacturing Industry and Foreign Capital

As we have seen, in the absence of an indigenous production complex for computer components, most Indian computer firms resorted to screwdriver operations – importing and assembling knock-down kits from abroad. The most complicated element in the process was adding the company's logo and the 'Made in India' seal.[24] Even for the larger firms, the most demanding element came with the after-sales software services and maintenance.[25] While on paper the Minicomputer Policy may have seemed to be bolstering domestic computer production, the 'manufacturing' firms, given the negligible value they added, were more akin to informal retail outlets for foreign companies.

6.4.3 Relations Between the Local Software Services Industry and the Installed Computer Hardware Base

A computer hardware base with bundled software impedes the growth of independent software services firms.[26] Most countries in the world in the early 1980s used computers with bundled software. This was because nearly all computer manufacturers bundled their software. After all, for a mass producer of computers this made commercial sense: writing software might require initial effort and expense; but once written it can be installed on all your computers at no added cost and sold thousands of times over. India, however, was an exception.[27] Its installed computer hardware base was primarily unbundled. The imported knock-down kits did not come with any software. Moreover, all of India's computer manufacturers (including the larger firms such as Wipro, HCL and Sterling) were petty producers by international standards. This meant that they did not produce computers at the required volumes to recoup the costs of writing software and bundling it with the computer hardware. Unlike the mass producers of computers, it did not make commercial sense to bundle their hardware with software.

Just as bundling impedes a software services market, unbundled computers boost it. The flood of unbundled computers on the Indian market led to a massive surge in domestic demand by users (primarily Business Houses) for third-party software services providers. Two years earlier (1976), though this was completely unrelated, the DoE had relaxed the conditions of the Software Export Scheme and allowed firms signed up to the scheme to provide software services to domestic clients (in addition to meeting their export obligations). This allowed the experienced Indian software services firms established under the Software Export Scheme to serve the booming domestic market.

The results were jaw-dropping. Between 1981 and 1986 revenues accruing to the Indian software industry through domestic software services provision increased 30-fold. In contrast, revenues from software exports in the same period increased just over sevenfold.[28] The Minicomputer Policy had, inadvertently, catalysed the growth of the software services industry.

6.5   CONCLUSIONS

The law of unintended consequences suggests that, while an intervention may or may not achieve its intended result, it will invariably lead to other unanticipated outcomes. The Minicomputer Policy is a testament to this. It was designed and implemented to meet Business House computer requirements: the absence of an enforced licensing system and the allowance of a veiled import-intensive computer industry worked in their interests. And yet it inadvertently set in motion a chain of events which catalysed the Indian software services industry, as evidenced by Figure 6.1. Without the corrupt, deceit-laden Minicomputer Policy, it is safe to say that the Indian software services industry would not be the size and strength it is today. At the same time, had the policy been implemented correctly, there might have been a thriving computer manufacturing industry instead. The following chapter illustrates just how integral the Minicomputer Policy has been to making India home to one of the world's largest software services industries.

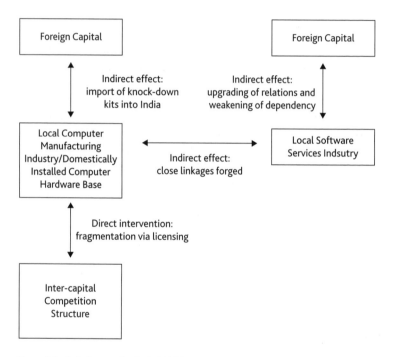

Figure 6.1   Relations at the End of 1985

7
Manna from Heaven: Satellites, Optic Fibres and the Export Thrust, 1986–2000

The most successful secessionist struggle in modern India has been that of the upper and middle classes from the rest of India.

Arundhati Roy[1]

7.1 INTRODUCTION

Extravagant consumerism in the 1980s is usually associated with the yuppie culture of New York and London. But the Indian middle classes were also going through a period of hitherto unprecedented consumer boom, albeit in a milder, less ostentatious way. This chapter explains how the causes and the consequences of this boom informed the shift in IT policy during this period, resulting in the unparalleled growth of software services exports.

7.2 THE WIDER CONTEXT: WHITE GOODS, BROWN SAHIBS – THE RISE OF INDIA'S CONSUMER SOCIETY

7.2.1 The Rise of the Indian Middle Classes and its Consequences

The burgeoning of the Indian middle classes has been one of the most significant demographic developments in post-independence India. By virtue of their privileged relations to the state apparatus, media and academia, as well as through sheer numbers, the middle classes in India from the 1980s onwards exerted tremendous political power. Their interests have shaped the character of the state's interventions across the economy since the 1980s in many respects.

According to the economists C.P. Chandrasekhar and Jayati Ghosh, the primary interest of this class lay in emulating the lifestyles of the Western middle classes.[2] In essence, this meant being able to access the same consumer goods – electronics, automobiles, white goods – as their counterparts in the United States and Europe.[3]

And to achieve this end, they sought the dismantlement of import controls on such goods.

Of course, pandering to these demands in their totality would have created serious political and economic problems. Any large-scale import liberalisation measures would have threatened the viability of the domestic manufacturing sector as a whole. Put simply, most domestic firms – in particular the politically influential Business Houses – would have been unable to compete effectively with foreign imports. Fierce resistance from these interests was to be expected. Moreover, in the absence of any counterthrust in exports, import liberalisation would, in turn, lead to chronic balance-of-payments problems.

How could this situation be resolved?

In the short term, a compromise between domestic manufacturing interests and middle-class demands was reached. Despite pressure from the affluent and aspirational groups, import controls on consumer goods were maintained. Instead, the consumerist desires of the middle class were to be met by the domestic firms, in particular the Business Houses.[4] At the same time, to keep the middle classes relatively contented, it was necessary to ensure the products were of comparable quality and affordability to foreign brands. This could only be achieved by allowing domestic firms to access advanced machinery and technologies cheaply from abroad.[5] Therefore the import of capital goods, intermediaries and raw materials was substantially liberalised.

Politically, the compromise seemed to work. Indian-manufactured consumer goods, such as Videocon television sets and Godrej refrigerators, temporarily satiated the middle class's consumerist demands. Domestic manufacturing industry – in particular the Business Houses – underwent huge expansion and diversification. However, from a broader economic perspective, the scenario was less rosy. The import intensity of the finished products plus the fact that they were being sold almost exclusively on the domestic market meant that balance-of-payments deficits started to grow substantially from the mid 1980s onwards. As a result, in order to maintain the politically comfortable situation discussed above and sustain the new pattern of national accumulation, the state had seriously to consider ways of boosting exports. As it was almost impossible to cajole Business Houses into the export market, the state, and in particular the Ministry of Finance, was on the lookout for other export opportunities.

7.2.2   An Additional Development: The 1980s Boom in the US Software Services Market

The USA always had by far the largest market in the world for software services. From the 1950s to the 1980s this had been due to the greater proclivity of US firms to use IT than their Japanese and European rivals (related to the labour market) and their preference for customised software (related to their greater size and organisational complexity, which meant software packages were not sufficient).

Two factors in the late 1970s and early 1980s further bolstered the US market's position as the number one software services market in the world. First, the PC revolution – which put small, affordable computers on the market – resulted in an ever more pronounced use of IT in corporate America.[6] Combined with the outsourcing phenomenon, which took off in the USA in the 1980s, this resulted in a boom in the software services market in the USA.

7.3   INTERESTS AND INTERVENTIONS: THE AMERICAN DREAM

While an increasing share of the Indian software firms' revenues was being generated by domestic services provision (courtesy of the Minicomputer Policy), they had remained active in the export market. The booming software services market in the USA had, therefore, quickly caught the eye of the established Indian software services firms. One development in particular very much excited them about their prospects in tapping this market. Progress in optic fibres and telecommunications satellites had meant that data could be transmitted across distance more reliably than ever before, in greater volumes, and at cheaper rates. Due to these recent advances in telecommunications technology, service provision by remote delivery had become a distinct possibility.[7] The remote-delivery model would allow for the more effective exploitation of wage differentials between software programmers in the USA and India than the body-shopping model.

Thus, if Indian software services firms could make the transition from services provision by body-shopping to remote delivery, their cost competitiveness in the US market vis-à-vis US software services firms would be significantly enhanced. However, for such a transition to occur, they would require access to the international telecommunications network. This could only be done via domestic telecommunications infrastructure linking them to the international network. And only the state could provide the enormous outlays this would require. Thus, the chief interest of Indian software services firms lay in ensuring state support for the provision of such infrastructure.

Luckily for the software firms, their interest in exports was perfectly aligned with the state's imperative to generate foreign exchange in the face of growing balance-of-payments deficits. As a result, the Indian state – and in particular the Ministry of Finance – pushed forward with an agenda to facilitate software exports from India to the booming US market.[8]

In 1987 the state announced that it would provide the necessary domestic telecommunications infrastructure to the software firms to boost exports.[9] By 1989 the infrastructure – via the International Packet Switching Service (IPSS) – was available to Indian software firms. Using such telecommunications links, Indian firms could now provide services by remote delivery. The new model was soon augmented by all manner of satellite links. Moreover, the state provided a number of other measures to aid Indian software firms in tapping export markets.[10] It sponsored marketing events with the aim of introducing firms to potential clients. The state was also involved in providing various credit and other financial and regulatory incentives to encourage firms to export software.[11]

The chief interest of the computer hardware manufacturers was very different. They had formed the Manufacturers' Association of Information Technology (MAIT) in 1983.[12] Its chief purpose was to articulate opposition to moves by the state towards the liberalisation of computer imports.[13] Lumbered with uneconomic scale, such firms were in no position to compete with the computer manufacturing behemoths of the USA and East Asia. The maintenance of the status quo was all they sought from the state.

However, their attempt failed. In complete contrast to the software firms, their demands were counter to the general direction being taken by the Indian political economy. Computer imports were liberalised year after year throughout the latter half of the 1980s, a policy perfectly in line with import liberalisation across a whole set of inputs into the production process. Just as the software exports helped to sustain the new pattern of national accumulation in India, so too did the relaxation of import controls on such an important intermediate good as computers. Indeed, balance-of-payments fears appeared to be the only restraint towards full-scale trade liberalisation of computer hardware.

7.4   WHAT HAPPENED? THE EMERGENCE OF THE MAJORS

The state's intervention in the IT industry during this period has been much feted. But is this justified? This section examines what the actual outcomes of the interventions were in terms of the key underlying economic relations of the industry.

7.4.1   Relations Between the Local Software Services Industry and Foreign Capital

As a direct result of the state's intervention in the provision of an appropriate telecommunications infrastructure, established Indian software services firms were now in a far more competitive position in terms of winning software services contracts in the US market. Via service provision by remote delivery, and building on their existing capabilities and profile in the US market, they could now outcompete most US firms in the lower-end market for software services. Contracts grew in size and number. And as the transition from body-shopping to remote delivery became more common through the 1990s, growth rates and profits also increased. In terms of industry growth rates from 1990 to 1997, the CAGR of total revenues was 24 per cent and that of exports was 33 per cent. These figures, while impressive, pale into insignificance compared to the growth witnessed at the end of the 1990s: between 1995 and 2002, the CAGR of revenues reached 30 per cent and that of exports an amazing 47 per cent. Profits also soared. According to the journalist Gubir Singh, by the start of the new century

> India's IT Inc. is literally on top of the world. The country's top 5 IT companies are among the most profitable and have the highest market capitalisations among all the full-fledged IT services firms worldwide. According to a NASSCOM analysis, Infosys is the most profitable among the world's purely IT services companies, followed by HCL Tech, Satyam, TCS and Wipro.[14]

Service provision by remote delivery also directly helped firms increase productivity and move up the value chain. Why was this? First, body-shopping had spawned much employee poaching by the TNC clients of Indian software firms. This was a problem in terms of firms moving up the value chain, where employee retention is of key importance. With body-shopping reduced, so too was poaching. The potential of firms to upgrade was, therefore, significantly bolstered. Second, remote delivery allows firms to keep most of its employees under one roof. This facilitates knowledge and experience transfer within firms. Again, this boosts a firm's ability to take on more complex projects. Thus, as service provision by remote delivery became more common, firms were able to win increasingly advanced and lucrative contracts. For example, in 1997/98, high-end applications accounted for just 5 per cent of the revenues of India's five largest software firms (and even less for the smaller firms); by 1999/2000, the figure had gone up to 26 per cent.[15]

Moreover, in this period three Indian software services firms started to grow more rapidly and upgrade their commercial relations with foreign capital faster than the other firms. These were TCS, Infosys and Wipro. Collectively, they had become the Indian Majors.

7.4.2   Relations Between the Local Computer Manufacturing Industry and Foreign Capital

In contrast to software services firms, the Indian computer manufacturers fared extremely badly under the state's new interventions. The larger firms, such as HCL, Sterling and Wipro, were the worst affected as it was their quality-conscious customers who were most likely to prefer imported computers. Sterling promptly went out of business, unable to compete with foreign imports. HCL and Wipro reorganised their hardware manufacturing divisions into official retail outlets for TNCCs. Wipro became a domestic sales outlet for Acer while HCL did the same for HP. Smaller Indian computer 'manufacturing' firms continued their import-intensive screwdriver operations. They maintained their already perilously low profit margins via resorting ever more to smuggling in components. By evading duties these firms were able to remain competitive to the most price-sensitive customers.

7.4.3   Relations Between the Local Computer Manufacturing Industry and the Local Software Services Industry

In the mid 1980s, the Indian software services firms had been part of MAIT. However, as the software firms felt their interests were not being articulated by MAIT, they resolved in 1987 to create their own association, NASSCOM.[16] At the time, this was seen as a negative development for the Indian IT industry. F.C. Kohli – head of TCS at the time – summarises this point of view:

> Frankly I was not happy about the formation [of NASSCOM]. The IT industry was nascent and I did not like fragmentation. I also believe hardware and software are two sides of the same coin. When the people who wanted to start NASSCOM came to see me, I blessed it but felt bad about it.[17]

The creation of NASSCOM proved to be the first step in the estrangement of relations between the two fractions of the IT industry. As the Indian software industry became more focused on exports to the USA, its interest in the domestic computer hardware installed base and the domestic computer manufacturing industry also declined. The transformation in the 1990s of both Wipro and HCL from computer manufacturers with significant software capabilities through after-sales services to fully fledged Indian software services firms with sidelines in computer retail epitomised the shift. Relations between the domestic computer manufacturing industry and both the local software services industry and foreign capital had now ceased to be a factor in the growth of the Indian IT industry.

7.5   CONCLUSIONS

For the IT industry, the 1990s was both the best and the worst of times, as evidenced by Figure 7.1. For the software industry, and

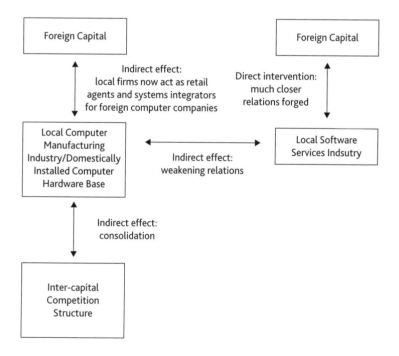

Figure 7.1   Relations at the End of 1999

in particular the three largest Indian software services firms – TCS, Infosys and Wipro – the state's facilitating role during the period had been manna from heaven (literally with regard to the satellite links). Without it, they would never have enjoyed the growth rates that they did. At the same time, any impartial observer of the Indian computer hardware industry would have been appalled at the state's total disinterest in developing such an important industry.

8
Passage to India: The Giants in the Land of the Majors, 2000–10

Earlier the government used to plan projects for drinking water, irrigation, roads, education and health. The focus of governments today is on projects like national highways, airports, modern sophisticated seaports, telecommunications and electricity for big industries. In other words, facilities that MNCs demand.

The National Alliance of People's Movement in India[1]

8.1 INTRODUCTION

When Aditya Chakrabortty, a columnist for the British broadsheet *The Guardian*, pondered whether the twenty-first century would be the Indian century, he was not alone.[2] For many, India and China are expected to dominate the twenty-first century in the way the USA and USSR dominated much of the twentieth century, and Britain and France before them.[3] Within these projections, the IT industry has been widely perceived as the flagship of this emerging Indian superpower. Dynamic, technologically savvy and massively internationalised, it seemed to embody perfectly the very features which would determine national success in the twenty-first century.[4] This chapter illustrates how and why such views are now outdated. If the industry ever was a flagship for national success, by 2010 it was rapidly sinking.

8.2 THE WIDER CONTEXT: AMONGST THE BELIEVERS – THE CAPITALIST CONVERSION OF INDIA

8.2.1 The Rise of Pro-liberalisation Capital

There have always been firms within the Indian political economy that have seen external liberalisation as a commercial opportunity.[5] However, such firms were outliers. They did not reflect the attitudes of their fellow firms in whichever industry or sector they operated. Rather, their approach can be attributed to the individual, idiosyncratic motivations of their founders. As such aspirations ran counter to convention, these 'renegade' firms were generally excluded from exerting any positions of authority within their respective industry associations, the official conduits to central government, and were therefore unable to influence national economic policy.[6] Frustrated by this, their ample energies were thus redirected towards building up close connections with regionalist parties with the aim of influencing policies in their commercial favour at a more local level.[7]

However, by the 1990s these renegade firms had become highly influential, not only in state government but also in New Delhi. This was due to the wider changes in Indian politics. In more detail, the breakdown of Congress's hegemony at central-government level throughout the 1980s had led to regional parties acting as kingmakers. They now had the power to make or break coalitions and hence were pampered accordingly. Many top government posts were awarded to the major players in regionalist parties.[8] In the words of one political scientist, the result was that India had 'national governments dominated by regional leaders'.[9] While many amongst the Indian elite found the rise of what they deemed provincial bumpkins to positions of great power distasteful, the renegade capitalists were busy toasting their success: by enjoying close relations with these regional leaders and bankrolling the parties they represented, they had entered the corridors of real power in India, partially usurping the Business Houses in the process. They would now be able to promote economic policies centred on liberalisation in their own favour.

8.2.2 Wider Attitudinal Changes Amongst Indian Capital

The growing political influence of the pro-liberalisation fraction of Indian capital induced attitudinal changes in the wider capitalist circles in two ways.

First, the self-appointed leaders of the new pro-liberalisation capitalist class, emboldened by their meteoric rise in political influence, propagated a new business ideology – or, more accurately, an attitude – across wider swathes of the capitalist class. This attitude had three main tenets, each drawn from the regional business classes' own experiences and self-serving mythologies. Tenet one was an aversion to state regulation and control, reflecting their deep-seated resentment of state interventions which they saw as favouring the Business Houses. Related to this, tenet two was firmly against any form of discriminatory approach to capital, be it large, small or foreign. This incorporated their own willingness to collaborate with foreign capital, often in opposition to the Business Houses. And tenet three was a supreme belief in the driving force of entrepreneurialism as the key for development, a result no doubt of their own background as successful first-generation businessmen. In short, the ascendant attitude was that globalisation should not be feared but embraced, and this attitude was readily transplanted onto other fractions of Indian capital.

Second, the 1991 IMF-imposed reform agenda was politically and ideologically important; but real, substantive economic liberalisation would be driven by domestic political economy, not international diktats. It was the political power of pro-liberalisation capital, not the IMF, which encouraged Business Houses to realise that resistance to liberalisation was futile; that the dismantlement of their market protection was only a matter of time; and that the pertinent questions over greater trade and investment liberalisation would be 'when' rather than 'if', and in whose benefit. The acceptance that the domestic market would no longer be their sole preserve prompted Business Houses to start seriously considering the export market as a new terrain for industrial expansion. Globalisation came to be seen by the Business Houses as a potential lifeline to continuing viability rather than the haunting spectre it had once been. As such, resistance to liberalisation dwindled and the Business Houses even started to preach the mantra of globalisation.[10]

This attitudinal shift amongst Indian capital was captured by the acclaimed political scientist Partha Chatterjee, who observed that by the end of the 1990s 'there appears to be much greater confidence amongst Indian capitalists to make use of opportunities opened up by the global flows of capital, goods and services'.[11]

8.2.3   Wider Attitudinal Changes Amongst the Indian Middle Classes

According to Partha Chatterjee, by the beginning of the twenty-first century the views of the Indian middle classes towards the state and market had fundamentally changed from the heyday of dirigisme in the 1970s.[12] The middle classes now revered the market and the private sector, which they saw as guided by 'professionalism and commitment'. And in contrast, the state had come to be seen as 'ridden with corruption and inefficiency'. There were three reasons for this.

First, the Indian middle classes had become intoxicated, much like the wider Indian capitalists, by the preachings of the pro-liberalisation firms. Second, they had also become increasingly Americanised via contact with the USA, primarily through relatives residing in the country.[13] Politically, this has led to the majority of middle-class Indians buying into the USA's neo-liberal view of the state and the economy.[14] Third, there had been the active promotion of a neo-liberal world view in India via both the media and academia. The Indian economist Biplab Dasgupta referred to this as the 'New Political Economy'.[15]

This had two implications for government policy. One relates to party politics. By the turn of the century, the Indian middle classes had a political influence far in excess of their numbers. This meant that their views and opinions shaped party manifestos and, in turn, policy agendas. The second implication concerns their more subtle influence on the policymaking process. The state apparatus in India was almost exclusively populated by the middle classes. Hence their views as a class could not help but shape the way IT policy was formed, even if the primary determinants remained economic forces and power configurations. The capitalist conversion of India played a key part in why and how the state would intervene in the IT industry in India in the first decade of the twenty-first century.

8.3   INTERESTS AND INTERVENTIONS: SOFTWARE AS SOFT POWER – THE RISE OF NASSCOM

The dominant interests in Indian IT policy in this period were the world's four largest software services firms: IBM, EDS, Accenture and Cap Gemini, collectively referred to as the Global Giants. Such interests emerged in the face of, and were forged by, the competitive challenge posed by the Indian Majors.[16] By effectively harnessing both India's skilled technical talent and its abundance of cheap English-speaking labour in a pioneering remote-delivery model, the Indian Majors were increasingly able to out-compete the Giants for lucrative contracts.[17] The only way for the Giants to offset the Majors' competitive advantage was, in essence, to emulate them.[18] Their interests were thus twofold: first, ensuring that they would have the same access to India's technical and English-speaking labour as their Indian rivals; and second, that they would have equal access to other supporting measures (that is, they would not be discriminated against).

In order to achieve these interests, the Giants first took control of the ostensibly 'national' industry association, NASSCOM. This was relatively easy to do due to the attitudinal shift amongst Indian capitalists. Stemming from the non-discriminatory attitudes of the Indian software capitalists, NASSCOM's membership criteria permitted TNC 'captives' in India to join.[19] Essentially, this meant TNCs would become members, as captives are not independent of their parent firm. Also, crucially, it allowed TNCs to vote for candidates in the strategy and policymaking body of NASSCOM, the Executive Council.[20] Aided by a voting system which tied the number of votes a firm had to its size, the TNCs, and in particular the Giants, were quickly able to exert domination over the Executive Council and therefore NASSCOM's agenda.[21] Reflecting this new locus of power, the TNC forum within NASSCOM was closed down in 2005, testimony to the fact that the entire association had become a TNC forum writ large.[22]

With the Giants in control, NASSCOM's focus and direction promptly changed. Prior to the Giants' takeover, the association had focused on what could broadly be referred to as a strategy of 'India Inc.', centred on supporting the growth of Indian software firms. This primarily involved informing foreign governments and corporations about the possibilities and benefits of awarding software services contracts to Indian software firms. Under Giant control, NASSCOM replaced its strategy of 'India Inc.' with that of 'Destination India'.[23] This new strategy concerned itself with facilitating a 'business-friendly' environment for attracting and maintaining IT-related FDI. In short, NASSCOM changed from lobbying foreign governments on behalf of Indian software services firms to lobbying the Indian government on behalf of foreign firms.

And NASSCOM soon proved to be very adept at 'lobbying' the Indian government on behalf of the Giants. This was due to three factors. First, the continued year-on-year double-digit growth of the software services industry in India had made the industry important – economically and ideologically – in sustaining the national pattern of accumulation. As such, recommendations purporting to sustain the industry's growth would now be afforded a high priority within the state apparatus.[24] Second, from 2000 onwards NASSCOM had taken over from the DoE as the chief purveyor of research and information on the industry. This was due to the middle-class character of the state and that class's recently acquired deference to big business. The DoE bureaucrats saw in NASSCOM a research and policymaking body that was superior to itself and happily acquiesced to playing second fiddle to it.[25] This meant that NASSCOM had a virtual monopoly on IT policy recommendations to the state. Third, again due to the middle-class character of the state, NASSCOM's recommendations were accepted as insightful, genuine and correct. The growing TNC contingent on the Executive Council, rather than raising questions as to the 'national' character of the association, instead reinforced the respect that NASSCOM's 'findings', 'analysis' and 'recommendations' found within the state apparatus.

NASSCOM's lobbying capabilities can be seen in the following two examples.

The first NASSCOM-instigated intervention was in the state's granting of concessions on ITES exports. NASSCOM had used (and abused) its monopoly on policy advice to the Indian state to make the case for these concessionary extensions.[26] It did this by claiming that without such concessions being granted, not only would no more new captives be established in India (with negative implications for the growth of the industry) but that the captives already operating in India might close down their operations.[27] With no alternative voice pointing out that existing captives were making an insignificant contribution to the industry revenues and that India's edge over all other rival offshore locations meant that it could enact high corporate taxes and still be the premier destination, the state acquiesced.[28]

The second NASSCOM inspired 'intervention', while less noticeable, was far more significant. When the Giants' captives started to engage in practices which, while beneficial to the Giants, were hugely detrimental to the industry overall (as is elaborated upon in the following section), NASSCOM was able to obfuscate both the cause and the effect of the problem, essentially blocking any intervention by obscuring the need for it.[29] The association incorrectly attributed the effect – that is, the industry's haemorrhaging growth – as an outcome of dwindling global demand for software services. Again, with no one questioning NASSCOM's wisdom, this view has been accepted uncritically, despite the fact that the Indian software firms' problems began in 2007, a year before the start of the global economic downturn. Moreover, rather than flagging up the problems with the practices of the captives, the association has exaggerated their benefits.[30] Again, despite their limited evidence base, few have dared question NASSCOM's assertions, and the notion of the captives being unequivocally good for the industry has remained conventional wisdom.

8.4   WHAT HAPPENED? FROM BIG DREAM TO MAJOR NIGHTMARE

By the late 1980s the domestic manufacturing industry and installed computer hardware base ceased to be important elements within the Indian IT industry. The key focus was on the commercial relations between the local software services industry and foreign capital. However, with the establishment and scaling up of the Giants' captives in India from the early years of the twenty-first century onwards, a new dimension was added: competition in the Indian labour market for talent.[31] This section examines how the competitive relations between Giants and Majors in the Indian labour market impacted on the latter's ability to upgrade continuously their commercial relations with foreign capital.

8.4.1 Productivity Hikes, 2000–05

The competition in the domestic labour market between Giants and Majors initially induced the Indian Majors to move up the value chain. This was because between 2000 and 2005 none of these firms engaged in poaching practices from each other, for two reasons. First, the Majors had long since settled on informal anti-poaching agreements amongst themselves, acknowledging that the costs of poaching far outweighed the gains.[32] Second, the Giants, who could, in theory, reap all the benefits of poaching while facing none of the costs (given their superior ability to attract and retain talent), also refrained from such practices during this period.[33] They were just beginning to enter India, had not yet secured NASSCOM, and did not want to trigger any antipathy to their expanding presence.[34]

Without poaching, competition took place in graduate-level recruitment, a battle for the best emerging talent.[35] To access the talent and ensure that the Giants did not cream off the best, the Majors were forced to raise their entry-level salaries. The commercial imperatives of ensuring they then got 'their money's worth' from such graduates impelled the firms to embark on significant organisational efforts to improve productivity.[36] In particular, serious investments were made in staff training, quality control and other human-resource practices.[37] The transfer to India of service provision that would have been previously carried out onsite was actively encouraged, as not only did it better utilise India's labour cost advantages, it also generated better intra-firm learning and knowledge transfer.[38]

These changes transformed the Indian software services firms, catapulting them up the value chain. Software services contracts of upwards of $50 million accounted for only 1 per cent of industry revenues in 2002, but had risen to 7 per cent by 2006.[39] According to NASSCOM, 'a trend had emerged whereby [Indian software services] firms were increasingly winning multi-year, multi-million dollar contracts with global firms'.[40] SMEs too were identified in the same NASSCOM paper as maintaining high growth rates and expanding their customer base. It was therefore not surprising that in 2005 NASSCOM predicted that Indian software firms 'are expected to fuel the overall momentum [of the IT industry in India] into the next decade'.[41]

8.4.2   Poaching Practices and the Feeder System, 2005–10

In 2005 it was not only NASSCOM that felt that the Indian software services firms were destined for greatness. Investors also shared their sentiments, sending the Majors' market capitalisations to all-time highs.[42] Even the usually cautious CEOs of the Majors began to emit triumphalist noises. However, the aura of optimism very quickly evaporated. Having secured their control of NASSCOM, and through NASSCOM the IT policy agenda, the Giants felt suitably emboldened to change tack in their recruitment. They stopped employing entry-level professionals and started poaching experienced employees of other software firms, in particular from Indian Majors.[43] An unoffical feeder system quickly materialised whereby the Majors and other Indian software firms trained their employees only for the best and brightest to be poached by the Giants after a number of years.

The impact of this on the Majors was catastrophic. In their quest to compete with the Giants in the top tier of the software services industry, the retention of staff was vital. Smaller Indian firms providing less sophisticated software services and ITES could afford to lose employees, as their replacements required less training. The Majors did not have that luxury. According to Gartner, the UK-based management consultancy, 'higher skilled IT professionals such as project managers and systems architects take years to cultivate and mature'.[44] So the loss of these employees was a major blow to the Majors.

The effects played out in the wider competition between the Majors and the Giants. The Majors, wracked as they were with already high and growing attrition rates, struggled to move into the highest echelons of the software services market. In contrast, the Giants successfully entered the product market in lower-end IT services previously monopolised by the Indian Majors in the 1990s and the early years of the twenty-first century. The journalist Subir Roy summarised the situation thus: '[A] perception is growing that the [Giants] are doing better in acquiring what they earlier lacked – cheap offshore capability – than the [Majors] are in their quest for deep consulting capabilities'.[45] After facing a substantial threat just a few years earlier, by 2010 the Giants were firmly back in the driving seat in the global software services industry. Their control of NASSCOM had been pivotal.

8.5   CONCLUSIONS

The period between 2000 and 2010 witnessed an unprecedented inflow of IT-related FDI. It has been venerated by many who have perceived this as evidence of the industry's development.[46]

However, as this chapter has shown, this is an overly simplistic conclusion. This influx has led to increasing problems for the Indian Majors, as illustrated in Figure 8.1. As a result of the recruitment practices of the Giants, the Majors struggled to break into the highest echelons of the software services industry. Chapter 9 examines what the future holds for the Majors and the wider software industry in India.

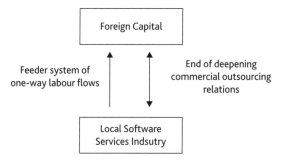

Figure 8.1   Relations between Giants and Majors in 2010

Part 3
The Analysis

9
The Indian Mutiny: From Potential IT Superpower to Back Office of the World

The Government of India has resolved to make India a global IT super power and a front runner in the information revolution.

Government of India[1]

A Planning Board ... can be taken over by the dominant interests, its activities turned into a sham, its existence used to nurture the illusion in the underlying population that something constructive is being done about economic development.

Paul Baran[2]

9.1   INTRODUCTION

At the turn of the century some economists were keen to diminish the achievements of the Indian software industry. The software programmers were mischaracterised as 'call-centre coolies' and the buildings in which they worked were referred to as 'white-collar sweatshops'. Moreover, the trade in services was portrayed as a twenty-first century digital equivalent of the nineteenth-century textiles trade, in which India exported raw materials and imported back finished goods.[3] Such views were wrong. The tremendous commercial and technical advances achieved by the Indian software services firms in the 1990s had rendered the notions of call-centre coolies and cyber-colonialism outdated. Strangely enough, however, by 2020 they may be apt. The software services industry is now in full-scale regression, threatening to transform the IT industry into a back office of the world. This chapter will explain how and why, and what might be done to reverse this prospect.

9.2   IN INDIA BUT NOT OF INDIA: THE SOFTWARE INDUSTRY IN 2020

Despite the global economic downturn there does not appear to be any let-up in the influx of IT-related FDI into India nor the scaling-up of existing TNC 'captives' already in the country. Incredibly, between 2008 and 2011 over 200 new captives were established in India.[4] Moreover, Accenture, IBM and Cap Gemini have added tens of thousands of employees to their already enormous Indian workforces in the same period. In line with the continuing influx, wages for employees in the industry have continued to soar, while TNC poaching has continued unabated.

This has had a damaging effect on the Indian software SMEs. For the first time since its creation, NASSCOM membership fell in consecutive years between 2007 and 2009.[5] This reflects the exit from the industry of many SMEs which were unable to remain commercially viable as wage inflation cut into their cost advantage, while poaching prevented them from achieving the productivity hikes necessary to offset the erosion of competitiveness brought about by salary rises. Unbelievably, the wage inflation had not out-priced them vis-à-vis rival firms from the developing world – for a number of reasons, such firms do not exist.[6] Rather, the level of wage inflation in India over the past decade has been so great that it has eroded the cost advantages such firms enjoyed over their US and European rivals.[7]

From a development perspective, however, the key concern is the effect the scaling-up of the Giants' captives is having on the Majors. After all, given that the three Majors are responsible for nearly 50 per cent of the industry's software services exports, and more than 25 per cent of the industry's revenues overall, any slowdown in their growth will have significant ramifications for the wider software industry in India.[8] The omens do not look good. As a result of the Giants' poaching, the Majors' growth has slumped, while attrition rates have soared.[9] Related to this, their ability to compete with the Giants in the higher-end software services tier has become a concern.

As a response to these conditions in the Indian labour market, the Majors have not expanded operations in India, preferring expansion abroad.[10] Infosys has recently established six new delivery centres in the developing world (four in China, one in Mexico and one in Brazil). TCS has followed suit, establishing three delivery centres in China and three in Mexico. The rationale is clear: to tap more stable (that is, poaching-free) labour markets. It remains to be seen if this strategy will keep the Majors competitive, let alone facilitate their entry into the highest echelons of the software services industry. However, even if the strategy is ultimately successful for the Majors in terms of commercial success, it is of limited benefit to the development of India. This is because, due to the various concessions granted to the software industry, employment generation in India is the Majors' most significant contribution to the country.

The implications of the demise of the Majors is immense. It presents a regression in the capabilities of the software industry in India. In more detail, the industry will rapidly be transformed from being a sector centred on Indian software firms primarily exporting IT services, to being an industry dominated by TNC captives engaged in the export of ITES (either as part of BPO operations or purely in-house). This change from domestic to transnational ownership is enough, of course, to infuriate those of a purely nationalistic point of view. However, there are three more important, non-nationalist reasons why this shift is a concern for the long-term development of the industry, as well as for India more broadly.

First, such a shift puts an end to the continuing commercial and technical advance of the Indian software services industry. While the further development of the Indian Majors offers much scope for wider evolution of the Indian software services industry, an industry centred on TNCs forecloses this opportunity. This is because higher-end software services still require onsite delivery, presenting natural barriers to Giants delivering higher-end software services from India. A far more likely scenario under a Giants-dominated industry is of the most talented Indians within a captive being 'delivered' to where the high-end software services are being carried out.

Second, a captive-dominated industry primarily exporting ITES is far less embedded in the economy and therefore less developmental as well as more unstable. This is for a number of reasons. First, TNCs are likely to see their captives in India – no matter how large – as peripheral to their core, higher-end service operations. They would thus not think twice about closing or downsizing their operations in India and moving them to another destination (off-offshoring) should conditions warrant it.[11] In contrast, the delivery centres in Bangalore, Chennai and Mumbai of the Indian Majors are the central nodes of their entire global operations and closing them would be unthinkable (even if the current expansion is primarily occurring abroad).[12] The risk of off-offshoring is increased by TNCs primarily being engaged in ITES exports. As ITES requires labour with fewer skills and less training, there are far more destinations for TNCs to relocate to.[13] With software services exports, the pool is far more limited.[14] Moreover, an ITES industry is also prone to automation due to the ease with which, say, a call-centre employee can be replaced by automated self-service customer interaction technology.[15]

Third, the shift from local firms to TNCs has a number of deleterious effects on the wider Indian economy. Due to the repatriation of profits by TNCs, there will be considerable leakage from the economy of the foreign exchange generated by the industry. In addition, due to the intra-firm migration practised by the Giants, such an industry will exacerbate the brain drain, leaving an acute shortage of highly skilled persons in India.[16] And finally, the Indian state and Indian firms will be forced to rely on Giants rather than local firms for their large IT projects.[17] This will significantly raise the costs of such projects, possibly to prohibitive levels, and thereby further impede the diffusion and adoption of IT across the country.

In short, if IT policy remains as it is, then the Indian software industry will be transformed from an export-driven industry based around nationally owned firms with potential positive externalities for the rest of the economy, to a low-skilled back office for the world's TNCs, vulnerable to off-offshoring and automation, and damaging to the wider economy.

9.3   POACHER AS GAMEKEEPER: EXPLAINING THE STATE'S INACTION

The state is doing nothing to address the emerging character of the industry, despite the wide-ranging negative ramifications it bodes. The situation reflects the state's reliance on NASSCOM for policy direction, as discussed in Chapter 8. As NASSCOM is dominated by the Giants, who are benefitting from the current system, it is not in the association's interest to draw attention to the problems of the industry and the failings of IT policy.[18] Instead, NASSCOM has been quick to attribute the slowing growth of the Indian IT industry to the global economic downturn, while conveniently failing to recognise a more profound structural crisis caused by the influx of IT-related FDI and the associated issue of poaching by TNCs.[19] The blocking role of NASSCOM has been used to great effect.

What is less understandable than NASSCOM's biased, pro-TNC reading of the situation in which the industry currently finds itself is the lack of a revolt within NASSCOM from the 80 per cent of its members who are not TNCs.[20] Why have the Indian software SMEs and Majors not mobilised, either to demand a change in NASSCOM's agenda or to form a breakaway group?

The software SME's inaction is due to the belief that NASSCOM reflects their interests and is addressing their needs. This false consciousness can in the main be attributed to NASSCOM's establishment of the Emerge Forum in 2007. Ostensibly, the forum is 'to help senior management of SME organisations exchange ideas, learn from other decision and opinion makers and use [this information] to improve their business'.[21] And through its 'killer workshops', 'Apstorms' and 'must-attend conferences', Emerge certainly gives the impression that NASSCOM is doing something for the SMEs.[22] Its web pages are eye-catching and the language deployed is dynamic and motivational. And yet, for all the myriad of articles, reports and discussion boards, the key problems afflicting SMEs (such as high attrition rates and poaching) are never acknowledged, let alone analysed and addressed.[23] For the cynic, Emerge appears less like a learning forum and more like a digital-age equivalent of the Roman Empire's bread and circuses, duping the SME 'masses' into thinking NASSCOM represents their interests.[24]

A lack of savoir faire cannot be used to explain the Indian Majors' inaction over NASSCOM's policy agenda. Both Narayan Murthy and Azim Premji, founders of Infosys and Wipro respectively, are shrewd operators; their commercial success evidence enough that they understand the way the business world works.[25] And sitting on the Executive Council, they are first-hand witnesses to the internal machinations of NASSCOM. Rather, their inaction is due to fear: first, a concern that any robust measures against TNC operations in India would be met with similar, quid pro quo moves against their activities in the USA and western Europe; second, a worry that stronger state regulation to address poaching might provide the basis for a much broader and concentrated intervention in the industry.[26] If the position of the Majors worsens further, which seems eminently possible, they may however be forced to become more assertive.[27]

9.4   NEVER MIND THE BUZZWORDS: A NEW AGENDA

This chapter has already analysed the consequences for the industry should IT policy remain centred on 'Destination India'. It has also explained why a shift in IT policy to address the problems has yet to occur. Issues of knowledge and ideology plus power and politics have combined to put a major fetter on necessary change. Nevertheless, the fetter is an unfortunate impediment rather than immovable ballast. While it can be safely assumed that the TNCs have cemented their hegemony within and through NASSCOM, it is highly unlikely that NASSCOM has, or ever could, capture the entire Indian state apparatus. With the myriad of competing interests and constituencies manifesting itself in the Indian state, the notion that one industry – even one as large as the software industry – or one association – even one as organised and effective as NASSCOM – could capture it in its entirety is absurd.[28]

Recent evidence supports such a view. In February 2011, the Indian finance minister, Pranab Mukherjee, announced that tax concessions for the software industry in India would not be extended into the new fiscal year. This decision was made in the face of the biggest NASSCOM lobbying campaign in the association's history. It therefore proves that NASSCOM's influence beyond the DoE is limited when it runs counter to greater concerns and interests (in this case, emerging budgetary issues and, relatedly, growing political instability). Moreover, while this decision had a fiscal rather than a developmental imperative, it opens up scope for a more concerted form of state intervention to address the crisis and safeguard the industry's longer-term development.

Whether the state will or will not fulfil its potential role as saviour of the industry is a conjecture beyond the scope of this book. It depends, in the first instance, on the balance of social forces in the Indian political economy. However, it also relies on the erosion of NASSCOM's monopoly over research on the Indian software industry and policy advice to the Indian state and the opening up of new policy conduits to the state, entertaining alternative policy agendas. Without multiple policy voices, NASSCOM will continue to be able to manipulate and subvert any alternative government agenda.

The central components of an alternative research agenda on the industry would need to address four key issues. These are outlined below.

- Poaching and the Feeder System
  The structural problems encountered by the industry have, at their root, the poaching system. It has prevented Indian software firms from migrating up the value chain. The TNC captives, in particular those of the Giants, have been the arch-practitioners of poaching. It is necessary to consider the following questions. Can self-regulation in the form of already existing anti-poaching agreements between Indian Majors be extended to incorporate the Giants, despite the asymmetries between the Majors and the Giants in their ability to attract and retain talent?[29] Can the state intervene via regulatory and legal means to tackle the TNC poaching system directly? Might

it be better to target energies away from tackling poaching head-on and instead consider ways in which the Majors could better retain talent?[30]

- Government Procurement
  The government is the biggest individual purchaser of IT products and services. A directed procurement strategy could thus play a major role in increasing the market share and developmental capabilities of the Indian Majors, particularly in providing a fillip to their higher-end capabilities in IT consulting.[31] It would also have the benefit of promoting IT adoption and diffusion across India and, given that Indian software services firms are cheaper than the Giants, it would be cost effective.[32] It is necessary therefore to consider the following questions. What type of IT projects might boost the Indian Majors' technical capabilities to allow them to compete at the highest levels of the software services industry? What type of IT projects might benefit the Indian economy and society? How might government procurement combine boosting the Indian Majors' software services capabilities with the IT needs of the country?[33]

- New Export Markets
  The Indian Majors are dependent on the US and western European markets. This dependency has forced them into a subordinate position within NASSCOM, as they are fearful that any opposition to the TNC-driven policy agenda of NASSCOM might lead to reprisals in the Western markets. The opening up of new export markets would lessen dependence on Western markets, releasing them from their subordinate position within NASSCOM and hence empowering them to promote more robustly measures which are in line with their own interests. It would also provide them with the commercial space to experiment with new business models, away from intense competition in Western markets.[34] It is necessary therefore to consider the following questions. Which export markets offer the best mid-to-long-term commercial opportunities per se?[35] Which of these markets are Indian firms best placed to tap?[36] Aside from subsidised marketing trips, are there any other ways to bring Indian software firms into contact with potential clients abroad? What help, if any, can the government of India provide?

- The Domestic Market
  Just as the exploitation of new export markets would provide
  the Indian Majors with the space to experiment with new
  business models and refresh their competitive advantages,
  so too might the domestic market. As Indian non-IT firms
  grow, they are likely to outsource more and more of their IT
  requirements. Thus, the domestic software services market
  provides, in theory, significant growth prospects. Moreover,
  the Indian Majors should have an advantage – via cultural
  affinity – in winning such domestic contracts. Important
  questions that need to be asked include the following. Is there a
  role for government in facilitating connections between Indian
  Majors and Business Houses seeking to outsource their IT
  requirements?[37] And can government procurement or subsidy
  play a middle-man role in facilitating linkages?

9.5   CONCLUSIONS

This chapter has shown that without a substantial change in IT
policy, the software industry's future looks bleak. However, while
the present conditions suggest that a policy overhaul is unlikely,
the cause is not lost. The state's intervention in the wrangle over
tax breaks shows that it has not been captured completely by
NASSCOM. It can, in theory, take a more robust interventionist approach to promote the development of the Indian software
industry in line with the wider development of the country. The
ability of IT policy to extricate itself from NASSCOM's influence
is a prerequisite for this. Four policy issues and associated research
agendas have been outlined which could help with this aim.
Ultimately, however, changes depend upon power configurations
within the industry as well as wider political conditions.

10
Lessons and Warnings: What Does IT Mean?

The ideas of the ruling class are in every epoch the ruling ideas.

Karl Marx[1]

10.1 INTRODUCTION

The book has provided a political economy account of the development of the IT industry in India, with special reference to the software services industry. This chapter draws out the wider lessons from the book's findings. The next section examines the appropriate broader role of IT policy in light of the industry's development. The section after that then discusses how the role of the Indian state in fostering economic development should be understood, given its interventions in the country's IT industry. The final section considers how the Indian software industry fits into the wider Indian political economy, pondering whether the industry really is a boon to Indian development, as most observers claim.

10.2 DON'T BELIEVE THE HYPE: THE ROLE OF IT IN DEVELOPMENT

There was a time when IT was seen solely as a facilitator of development via its diffusion into a developing country's economy. It was perceived as an intermediary technology, whose adoption by local firms would boost their productivity and hence their competitiveness. This, in turn, would help a country develop economically. However, this was a time when the advances made by the Indian software industry were little known outside of the DoE, the Indian software firms, and IT managers in TNCs, who were increasingly contracting software services to Indian firms.

Growing international awareness of the Indian software industry's 'success' over the past decade has, however, changed such views.[2] IT is now perceived by the international development agencies as an industry in its own right – in fact, an export-oriented software industry like that found in India is seen as *the* industry with major growth potential in the twenty-first century, and therefore as one to be cultivated and promoted by the state.[3] The World Bank, in particular, has been keen on projecting this view, claiming that the Indian IT industry could represent an entirely new model of development.[4]

Either by design or coincidence, the neo-liberal myth of the Indian software industry's development has informed the policy template promulgated by the World Bank to developing-country policymakers. Thus, as most neo-liberal accounts exaggerate the significance of FDI and underplay the role of local software capital in the industry's development, the policy literature has stressed the virtues of creating a business-friendly environment for IT-related FDI.[5] In more detail, policy prerequisites for an appropriate business-friendly environment for an Indian-style software industry have included not only investment in human and physical infrastructure, but also tax concessions and various subsidies. Moreover, countries are advised not to differentiate and discriminate between lower-end ITES and higher-end software services. It is claimed that FDI in low-end ITES has the potential to develop into higher-end software services exports at a later point. And finally, it is claimed that IT-related FDI will have a positive effect on the wider economy.

There are four key lessons, derived from the development of the Indian IT industry, which undermine the World Bank's policy prescriptions.

- The first and most important lesson is that FDI, even in the form of ITES, is unlikely to materialise just by establishing a 'business-friendly environment', complete with cheap but skilled labour, excellent telecommunications infrastructure and a whole panoply of tax concessions. IT-related FDI arrived in India for a number of idiosyncratic reasons. One factor was growing awareness by TNCs of India as a potential software platform through the services provided to them by Indian software firms.[6] Another cause was the growing perception within the United States of Indians as technically talented, due to the prominence of NRIs in the US high-tech industry. This prompted TNCs to consider offshoring to India to tap its labour pool.[7] Another determinant was that the Global Giants – the major TNC employers in the industry – arrived in India en masse to offset the competitive advantage of their emerging rivals, the Majors. And finally, offshoring depends on critical mass, where 'success' in attracting FDI creates a snowball effect, as happened in India at the turn of the millennium. Given the number of countries now offering themselves as offshore destinations, it is unlikely any one country can reach that critical mass needed to instigate a snowball effect.

- A second key lesson is that FDI in ITES will not necessarily lead to higher-end FDI. For example, most of the TNC 'captives' in India are still primarily engaged in the export of ITES from India. This is despite such captives having had a presence in the country for nearly a decade.[8] This should not be surprising. As already discussed in Section 9.2, there are a number of barriers to the transfer of higher-end work outside TNCs' home countries or major markets. It is far more likely that talented employees will be transferred back to the TNC's headquarters to work on higher-end projects than it is that higher-end projects will be transferred to the TNC captive in the host country.

- A third lesson is that FDI in ITES and IT will not automatically lead to greater IT diffusion across the rest of the economy and society. Instead, and even counter-intuitively, it will inhibit it. This is because part of the 'business-friendly environment' allegedly required to develop an Indian-style software industry is the strong enforcement of anti-piracy software laws. As software piracy is one of the key ways in which IT is diffused, any strict enforcement of anti-piracy laws will inevitably lead to less rather than more IT diffusion. India illustrates this clearly. As NASSCOM became dominated by TNCs (including Microsoft) the state zealously began to clamp down on software piracy.[9] As a result India has slipped in the World Bank's IT diffusion rankings.[10]

- A fourth lesson is that FDI in ITES and IT will not automatically lead to other positive externalities. The policies advocated by the World Bank – specifically tax breaks for exports and duty-free imports for computers – promote enclave-like behaviour by TNC captives.[11] A far more realistic scenario, based on the actual Indian experience, is that IT-related FDI will stifle and potentially suffocate any locally based, indigenous software industry via poaching.[12] And in the longer term, it will lead to a race to the bottom between countries vying to attract and retain FDI in ITES by providing ever greater subsidies and concessions.[13] In such a scenario, the only winners will be the TNCs.

However, not only do the book's findings in Part 2 cast doubt on the World Bank's policy agenda, they also undermine the notion that the Indian software industry can be emulated at all. That is, replication of the Indian software industry, in particular the software services industry (that is, large, nationally owned domestic firms exporting software services), is impossible due to the fact that Indian Majors enjoyed a number of advantages that emerging software firms from the developing world are no longer able to enjoy. These are listed below.

- The first advantage was that by the mid 1980s Indian software firms had both an international profile (particularly in corporate America) and advanced technical capabilities unmatched in the rest of the developing world. These unique features were due to the Software Export Scheme and (indirectly) to the Minicomputer Policy. This meant that the Indian software firms established in the 1970s and early 1980s had a virtual monopoly on the remote delivery of software services.[14] They faced no price competition from foreign companies, allowing them to penetrate Western markets very effectively and grow substantially. This commercial opportunity had ended by the mid 1990s.
- The second advantage was that the market the Indian Majors were penetrating so effectively in the late 1980s and early 1990s was growing extremely rapidly. This was due to the emerging business phenomenon of outsourcing all non-core firm operations (see Chapter 2). By plugging themselves into the growing market in IT services and IT outsourcing, Indian Majors were able to reap fully the fruits of such a seismic market expansion during that time period.[15] Now, however, this market is fully matured, offering no opportunity for more recently established software firms to piggyback on high industry growth rates.
- The final advantage for the Indian Majors in the 1980s was that they were entering a market for lower-end IT services that the Giants had, generally, eschewed.[16] Their primary competitors were small Western software services firms which did not have the resources to compete against the extremely cost competitive Indian Majors (recall that contracts in the lower-end IT services and IT outsourcing markets are primarily awarded on price). The absence of Giant competition meant that firms were better able not only to penetrate the markets,

but also to experiment with new business models in order to enhance productivity.[17] The absence of competition in this tier of the software services industry is no longer the case. The Majors and the Global Giants now provide integrated services from the highest to the lowest tiers of the software services industry.

As one can see, the Majors benefitted from an idiosyncratically shaped first-mover advantage at a time when the industry offered excellent growth prospects. Replicability is no longer possible.

10.3   BEYOND GOOD AND EVIL: THE ROLE OF THE STATE IN DEVELOPMENT

The myth of the Indian software industry's development has been used to sell the virtues of neo-liberalism in India. However, the actual development of the industry, based on a number of state interventions, offers three contrasting lessons regarding what role the Indian state might play in fostering wider Indian economic development. These are listed below.

- First and foremost, the development of the Indian software industry during the 1970s and 1980s demonstrates that the ISI period was not one of developmental disaster after developmental disaster.[18] Rather, while failures may have been commonplace, there were also real industrial and technical advances made during the period. Moreover, these advances were not a result of certain industries flying under the radar, but of active state intervention.[19] The growth of such industries, of which the Indian software industry is the most visible, in the so-called post-liberalisation era in India supports the research carried out by Harvard economists Dani Rodrik and Arvind Subramanium.[20] They identified that the current growth of the Indian economy rests primarily on sectors in which the Indian state intervened most heavily during the ISI period.[21]
- Second, the development of the Indian software industry in the so-called post-liberalisation era has continued to be heavily guided by the state's ongoing interventions. It is definitely not the case that the state has rolled back from the industry. Indeed, in terms of total state outlays on the industry (primarily via investments in physical infrastructure) and in the government's 'development' priorities, a strong case can be

made that the state has intervened *more* extensively following the 1991 liberalisation than before. This suggests that, for all the rhetoric of liberalisation, and despite the IMF and WTO diktats, the Indian state still continues to intervene in industries and sectors. The state's recent interventions in the software industry support the view of Professor Atul Kohli of Princeton University that the economic regime in India should be classified as pro-business rather than pro-market.[22]

- Third, the development of the Indian software industry from 1970 to 2005 highlights just how effective the Indian state *can* be in fostering development in industries. The Indian software industry would not exist in its current form (large, advanced and [still] dominated by local firms) without the state's support for Indian software firms, first via the Software Export Scheme in the 1970s, then from the late 1980s onwards via the provision of infrastructure, and other promotional activities. While not all its interventions in the industry have been developmental, the fact that so many have been amply demonstrates that the Indian state should not be considered 'the most dramatic case of a failed developmental state', as described by Professor Richard Herring.[23]

In highlighting that state intervention, both now and in the past, is driving the country's most dynamic industry, the findings are far from salutary for those wedded to neo-liberalism in India. It would seem obvious that the state should intervene more substantially across broader swathes of the Indian economy to promote sectors and industries in which the social returns for growth are far greater than in the software industry. However, as illustrated throughout this book, the sectors in which the state intervenes, as well as the manner and form of the interventions, are not dependent on a technocratic reading of the situation and the goal of the 'national interest' (whatever that may be). Rather, they are based on the motivations of, and power configurations between, interests attached to particular sectors of the economy, and how these feed into, and reflect, the balance of social forces in both the domestic and international political economy. Whether or not the Indian state intervenes more widely depends on a myriad of machinations which cannot be conjectured on at this point.[24] What the findings show, however, is that the rolling-back of the state cannot be justified solely through the academic argument that it is inherently defective or via the legal point that it breaks with international rules and regulations.

10.4 GOLDEN CALF OR TROJAN HORSE? THE ROLE OF THE SOFTWARE INDUSTRY IN THE INDIAN ECONOMY

While NASSCOM has, over the past half-decade, played a significant role in impeding the long-term growth prospects of the Indian software industry, it now looks set to go one step further. Its current 'priority issue' of H1-B visas (short-term work visas for highly skilled migrants working in the USA) is threatening to undermine the wider Indian economy as well. The situation is as follows. NASSCOM claims that maintaining access to large numbers of H1-B visas is vital to the growth of the Indian IT industry. The Indian state, populated as it is by the middle classes, has uncritically accepted this claim. Moreover, given the priority weighting afforded to the Indian software industry by this class, the state has prioritised visa access in all its economic negotiations.

Consider, first, India's multilateral relations. The pursuit of better access to visas for short-term skilled migration has led the Indian negotiating team at the WTO to side with the developed world in promoting full-scale liberalisation of services. Such liberalisation measures are not necessarily in the interests of the rest of the Indian economy, nor indeed of any developing economy. This is why India was the only major developing country to side with developed countries in these negotiations.[25] Even more disconcerting is that H1-B visas have started to dominate Indo-US economic negotiations. Access to H1-B visas is now being used by the US government as a key bargaining chip to gain better access to the Indian market in industrial and farm goods.[26]

The situation is bordering on the farcical for two reasons.

First, the belief that sectors of the Indian economy (industry, agriculture and non IT-related services) should be sacrificed for the sake of the software industry could only be justified from a development point of view on one premise: that the software industry has the ability to transform the Indian economy from developing to developed. Such a transformation can only come via the generation of jobs that pay above subsistence for hundreds of millions of Indians. Can the software industry contribute significantly to this? A cursory glance at the figures suggests that this many jobs will not be generated, directly or indirectly, by the software industry, no matter how rapidly it grows. For all the hype, the Indian software industry employs just 2.2 million people directly and a further 8.2 million indirectly.[27] Altogether this accounts for just over 2 per cent of India's total labour force.[28] Rather than through the expansion of the software industry, the necessary jobs will need to be generated by increasing agricultural productivity and expanding industry – precisely the two sectors which are most threatened by the Indian government's visa fixation.

Second, the very notion that the viability of the software industry in India rests on visas is patently absurd. There is no evidence whatsoever that the software industry requires plentiful access to them to survive. TCS, India's largest software firm, was not even amongst the top ten recipients of such visas in 2009. Yet its exports to the USA did not suddenly vanish, but continued in much the same way as before. Local employment and advanced telecommunications mean that onsite work can be provided by non-migrants or reduced significantly. It is telling that only three of the top ten recipients of H1-B visas for Indian workers were Indian software firms. The rest were large Western TNCs, including three of the Giants.[29]

This suggests that NASSCOM is not just a tool of the Giants. Rather, its 'marketing' of access to the H1-B visas as a vital concern for the software industry indicates it has become a Trojan horse for Western capital more generally. That is, it is guilty of manipulating its position as 'strategic advisor' to the Indian state on IT policy and playing to the Indian middle class's obsession with the software industry to prise open the Indian economy. In this respect, the top brass in NASSCOM can be considered to be dot.compradors – native-born agents of foreign businesses – par excellence.

11
Conclusion: Of Compradors and Useful Idiots

In terms of resources of coal and iron and land for cotton-growing as well as in the supply of skilled weavers India should have been the seat of the first industrial revolution. But Indian armies had been defeated in 1757 by British armies and Indian merchants bought off by British traders. The textile industry of India, which had supplied all Europe with cotton goods up to the end of the eighteenth century, was destroyed by machine-made textiles, and as a British governor reported the result, 'the plains of Bengal were bleached white with the bones of the weavers'.

Michael Barratt-Brown[1]

Hegel remarks somewhere that all great world-historic facts and personages appear, so to speak, twice. He forgot to add: the first time as tragedy, the second time as farce.

Karl Marx[2]

Speaking at the NASSCOM Leadership Forum in Mumbai in February 2011, the Indian IT minister, Kapil Sibal, claimed that by 2020 revenues from the IT industry in India would top the $225 billion mark. The following day, his words were splashed triumphantly across the front pages of India's leading English-language newspapers.

This scenario epitomised the manifold problems of policy towards, and discourse on, the software industry in India. First, the $225 billion figure was not based on any of the government's own research on the industry, but was plucked from a report by NASSCOM, illustrating the dependency of the Indian state on the association. Second, the NASSCOM report in question had been published in 2009 and quickly discarded, given that its analysis had been rendered irrelevant by subsequent changes globally and sectorally. The use of a figure from such a report demonstrates either the state's total incompetence or its utter disingenuousness. Third, despite the unreliability of the figure, it was overwhelmingly endorsed by India's usually cantankerous and sceptical broadsheets, highlighting the media's sycophancy towards the industry.

The cumulative effect of the incompetence, disingenuous-ness and sycophancy surrounding the Indian software industry, encapsulated by Sibal's prediction and the media's response to it, has been to obfuscate its past, present and future developments. It is this situation that the book has sought to address by providing a clearer view not only of where the industry has come from but also of where it is going.

The first aim was to provide a detailed and accurate historical account of the industry's development from the 1970s up to the present day. Adopting a political economy framework, the book demonstrated, unequivocally, that state interventions have played an integral part in the industry's development. Moreover, it highlighted how geopolitics, class dynamics, vested interests and elite corruption have driven, and continue to drive, these interventions.

The second aim was to draw from the historical account a better understanding of the current role of the state in the industry, the rationale behind it and the effect it is having. The picture presented was sobering. The book highlighted how, for nearly a decade, IT policy has not only been unresponsive to the needs of Indian software firms but has, indirectly, undermined the attempts of the largest of these firms to migrate successfully into the upper echelons of the software services industry. The policy debacle is attributed to changes in the power configurations amongst interests with a stake in IT policy in India, in particular the shift in political influence from local software firms to the large Western IT firms. Without a significant change in IT policy, the industry will undergo a rapid and extreme form of underdevelopment.

The book's third aim was to outline a broader research agenda on the industry, with the intention of promoting a more effective form of state intervention. The book identified four areas in which greater research effort needs to be expended: the labour market for software professionals, in particular how best to tackle the debilitating poaching and feeder systems; the use of government procurement as a means of tying together greater IT usage in India and facilitating the upgrading of the Indian Majors; the identification of alternative export markets and the drawing-up of appropriate trade policy to tap them effectively; and, finally, it surveyed commercial opportunities within the domestic market.

However, the findings also raise broader and unexpected concerns. While the book noted that the wider vagaries of Indian political economy – from national security imperatives to middle-class consumer desires – shaped IT policy and the Indian software industry in the 1970s and 1980s, it also identified how this process has started to reverse itself, with the industry exerting increasing influence over the country in a myriad of ways. NASSCOM's manipulation of the H1-B visa issue to prise open various Indian agricultural and industrial markets, with ramifications across economy and society, is one example. The widespread support amongst the young, urban middle classes for such liberalisation measures (and for neo-liberalism in general), due to erroneous projections of the software industry as a product of economic liberalisation, is another.

These two wider trends have recently merged, with NASSCOM cleverly manipulating the pro-liberalisation sympathies of the middle classes to pressure the government into pursuing wider economic liberalisation, under the premise that failure to do so could jeopardise both the Indian software industry and the dynamism of the national economy. The validity of such claims is questionable in the extreme, and the fact that they have been articulated by a so-called national association controlled by a small clique of major Western firms adds to the surreal, through-the-looking-glass element of the situation. Thus, in a nod to Marx's quip regarding the path of history, in the name of progress and patriotism we now have the young, urban middle class – whose forefathers spearheaded the independence movement – pushing for policies which will succeed only in undermining economic development and national sovereignty.

In the smoke-and-mirrors world of the Indian software industry and the functioning anarchy of the country's wider political economy, there is no way of accurately guaging how these trends will eventually play out. Suffice it to say that the only certainties regarding the scenario painted above are that if Marx had been alive to observe it, he'd be toasting his prescient witticism; and if Gandhi hadn't been cremated, he'd be spinning in his grave.

Notes

GLOSSARY

1. The semiconductor industry is occasionally included as part of a wider computer hardware industry (and hence included under the IT industry umbrella). However, although semiconductors are important inputs in computer manufacture, in this book the semiconductor industry will not be included.
2. From the entry for Information Technology in the *Puffin Dictionary of Computer Words* (London: Penguin, 1983).
3. The inclusion of ITES under the IT industry umbrella term is for three reasons. First, most software services firms also provide ITES to their clients (see Chapter 2). Second, the revenues derived from TNC captives providing in-house ITES to their parent firm or customers are included in India within the total IT industry revenues. Third, while the technically accurate term IT–ITES industry has recently been promoted by the National Association of Software and Service Companies (NASSCOM), it will not be adopted in this book as it lacks global familiarity, popular usage and is also heavy on the eye.
4. For the Majors' contribution (47 per cent) to the industry's software exports, see Subir Roy, 'The Software Saga Should Continue', *Business Standard*, 23 July 2008. For the Majors' contribution (26 per cent) to the industry's overall revenues, see the OECD's *The ICT Sector in India: Performance, Growth and Key Challenges* (Paris: OECD, 2010): 41.
5. From the entry for outsourcing in *A Glossary of Computing Terms* (Toronto: Addison Wesley Longman, 1998).
6. From the entry for software in C.J. Meadows, *Dictionary of Computing and Information Technology* (London: Kogan Page, 1987).
7. There are three reasons why 'software services industry' is preferred over the other term used to describe such an industry, 'IT services'. First, the dominant operation in these firms remains the enhancement or design of customised *software* to clients and hence the term is more appropriate. Second, and related to this, the Indian firms such as Wipro, Infosys and TCS are primarily known in India and globally as 'software firms' or 'software services firms'. 'IT services industry' and 'IT service firms' are both relatively recent terms whose usage is restricted to industry insiders or business commentators. Third, the term 'IT services' is more open to conflation and confusion, as it is often understood as a specific type of service which does not incorporate IT consultancy or IT outsourcing.

A PRIMER

1. These sensationalist newspaper headlines associating Bangalore and software are not taken from some English language tabloid but from *The Guardian*, Britain's most intellectual and sombre broadsheet.

2. Over the past decade the city has even entered the lexicon via the neologism 'bangalored'. To be bangalored means to have one's IT-related job relocated to a developing country.

3. Bangalore was incorporated into the British Empire with the defeat of Tipu Sultan at the end of the eighteenth century. Given its high elevation, the climate was deemed well-suited to the British in India. As such, a large cantonment was built in Bangalore to house the British military forces, colonial administrators and commercial operators. As the British presence in India expanded, so did the cantonment: bungalows were established to house British colonial officers and their families. The British-inhabited part of the city began increasingly to resemble the English home counties. With the departure of most of the British presence following independence in 1947, the climate, leafy avenues and spacious bungalows began to attract India's affluent elderly, who saw the city as the perfect place to which to retire.

4. Shyam Somnadh, 'Let's Do a Bangalore: John Kerry', *Times of India*, 28 June 2004.

5. It is not just global leaders who believe Bangalore to be the centre of information technology. *New York Times* journalist and globalisation guru Thomas Friedman also seems to share the belief that Bangalore is pivotal to the brave new world of twenty-first century IT. In his seminal *The World Is Flat: A Brief History of the Twenty-First Century* (London: Allen Lane, 2005), Friedman famously begins his quest to understand globalisation while playing golf in Bangalore. He is asked to aim between the IBM and Microsoft buildings, upon which, he claims, it dawned on him that the world was embarking on a new phase in the global economy – the flat world.

6. Taken from extensive firm data in Suma Athreye's 'The Indian Software Industry', in Ashish Arora and Alain Gambardella (eds), *From Underdogs to Tigers: The Rise and Growth of the Software Industry in Brazil, China, India, Ireland and Israel* (Oxford: Oxford University Press, 2005): 14.

7. Ibid.

8. Chennai's base as India's most technologically sophisticated IT hub is in the main due to the linkages between the city's domestic electronics hardware manufacturing base established following independence and the software firms founded in the city several decades later. This is best evidenced by the Indian software firm DSQ, which, throughout the 1990s, was India's most innovative IT firm, pioneering both new business models and advanced technologies.

9. Suma Athreye, 'The Role of Transnational Corporations in the Evolution of a High-Tech Industry: The Case of India's Software Industry – A Comment', *World Development* 32 (3), 2004: 557.

10. The issue of perspective is also evident in the high profile in the West of the southern Indian city of Hyderabad. The city is frequently referred to in the British media as 'Cyberabad', a sobriquet acquired as a result of its image as a city awash with IT-related activity, and passed off as second only to Bangalore in India's software hub hierarchy. However, while it is the second most popular destination in India for the establishment of TNC captives, its contribution to the Indian software industry's revenues is less than 5 per cent. See Athreye, 'The Indian Software Industry': 14.

11. 'Newspeak' refers to state propaganda in George Orwell's novel *Nineteen Eighty-Four*, where inverted information was taken to its extreme, epitomised in the quote 'war is peace, freedom is slavery, ignorance is knowledge'.

12. Even respected commentators on the Indian software industry, such as Vivek Wadha, seem to believe that the Indian IT industry has its roots in call centres. In his 2010 article 'Indian Technology's Fourth Wave', available at www. businessweek.com/technology (last accessed 19 July 2011), Wadha claims that 'the Indian technology industry got its start running call-centres for companies in the West'. As Part 2 illustrates, Wadha is about two decades off the mark.

13. The revenues generated by call centres, either via BPO or captives, pale into insignificance vis-à-vis the revenues generated by IT consultancy, IT services and non-call-centre IT outsourcing. See Glossary and Chapter 2 for a more detailed explanation of how call centres fit into the wider Indian IT industry.

14. This can be disputed, however. An IPSOS Mori Poll in 2003 found that 74 per cent of the British public were unaware that many call centres had been offshored to other countries. The poll and report, titled 'Foreign Call Centres', is available at www.ipsos-mori.com (last accessed 19 July 2011). It would therefore seem that the furore that erupted in the United Kingdom in 2004 over call centres being transferred to India was not an organic response by the British public, but rather was whipped up by a jingoistic media. As a result of this, some call centres in India have tried to mask their locations by providing employees with accent training. Employees have also been given fake names so, for example, the Indian employee Rajesh becomes 'Roger' when providing call-centre services to Western customers. The psychological effect such aping is having on the employees is slowly being investigated; see S. Nadeem's *Dead Ringers: How Outsourcing Is Changing the Way Indians Understand Themselves* (Princeton, N.J.: Princeton University Press, 2011) for an interesting analysis.

15. This is particularly prevalent on the BBC News website (www.bbc.co.uk).

16. For one of the most extreme examples of this principle, see the great economic historian Alfred Chandler's 'How High-Technology Industries Changed Work and Life World-Wide from the 1880s to the 1990s', *Capitalism and Society* 1, 2006: 38. In this article Chandler assumes that the rapid growth of Japan's computer and microprocessor industries in the 1970s was due to the emigration to Japan of one US citizen, Gene Amdahl, who was previously IBM's lead chip designer. There is no mention of the role of the Japanese business groupings – the Keiretsu – in providing Japanese computer firms with a distinct advantage over firms in the West in maturing industries via favourable financing and procurement arrangements. In addition, if ties with the West are always positive, any breaking of such links must, then, be catastrophic. For example, Joseph Grieco, in *Between Dependence and Autonomy: India's Experience with the International Computer Industry* (Berkeley: University of California Press, 1984), argued that the Indian government's actions against IBM in the 1970s was a massive failure in policy.

17. Robert Miller, *Leapfrogging? India's Information Technology Industry and the Internet* (Washington, D.C.: World Bank, 2001): 15.

18. Chapters 2 and 8 provide evidence that the success of Indian software firms in Western markets induced the Global Giants to establish a significant presence of their own in India.

19. Since 2005 NASSCOM, the key processor of Indian IT industry data, has been reluctant to single out the contributions of TNCs to the industry's revenues. However, in its 2005 pre-Budget Memorandum it noted that 65 per cent of revenues in low-end IT-enabled services, such as call centres, came from TNCs, while Chandrasekhar and Ghosh, in 'Concentration in the Competitive Software

Business', *Macroscan*, 8 November 2006, put the TNC share of higher-end software services revenues at between 10 and 15 per cent. In short, TNC captives are increasingly monopolising the export of lower-end services, while Indian software firms are almost exclusively involved in the export of higher-end software services.

20. This is discussed in detail in Chapters 5 and 8.

21. See Chapter 5 for a detailed analysis of the role of IBM in India in the 1960s and 1970s.

22. See Nandita Datta, 'The Great Gamble', *Outlook Business*, 18 September 2010.

23. Abishek Pandey, Alok Aggarwal, Richard Devane, Yevgeny Kuznetsov, *India's Transformation to Knowledge-based Economy: Evolving Role of the Diaspora* (Washington, D.C.: World Bank, 2004): 17.

24. The author first came across the term 'brain gain' at the EU–India Roundtable Meeting at the European Commission, Brussels in November, 2007. Professor Vijay S. Pandey referred to 'brain gain' after the author enquired as to what he thought of the deleterious effects of the skilled emigration from India in the country's development.

25. See S.P. Sukhatme, *The Real Brain Drain* (Orient Longman: Hyderabad, 1994) for an excellent overview of the Indian brain drain and its effects.

26. According to NASSCOM, 25,000 scientists and engineers returned to India between 2001 and 2004. However, NASSCOM also acknowledges that only 30 per cent of these returnees were Indians with US citizenship or permanent residency (i.e. green card holders); the rest were returning after holding short-term working visas, most likely for an Indian software firm. This suggests that only approximately 8,000 people can be considered genuine returnees during this period. While this may still sound like a large number, if compared with the numbers of skilled Indians emigrating to the USA, it pales into insignificance. See Ashok Desai's 'India', in Simon Commander (ed.), *The Software Industry in Emerging Markets* (Cheltenham: Edward Elgar, 2005): 39 which puts the figure of skilled Indians emigrating to the USA in 2001 on short-term visas alone at 136,000. The number of skilled Chinese emigrating to the USA was just 12,000.

27. See Desai, 'India,' for an excellent account of the career trajectory of an Indian software engineer, in which the final stage is a return to India to manage a US subsidiary.

28. See Pandey et al., 'India's Transformation': 17.

29. This will be discussed in detail in Chapter 5.

30. The five largest Indian software firms are TCS, Wipro, Infosys, Satyam and Patni Computer Systems. Of these only Satyam, established in 1987, does not have its roots in the 1970s. Infosys, while established in 1981, was founded by disgruntled employees of Patni Computer Systems (established in 1978).

31. The literature from which these terms have been plucked is critically reviewed in Chapter 3.

32. Contradictory policies include further import liberalisation for computers and developing a hardware industry, reducing employee attrition and increasing the TNC presence, and encouraging broad-based economic development while advocating allocation of greater educational resources to IT colleges.

33. As of 2009, 2.2 million people were employed directly by the IT industry in India and 8.2 million indirectly. Cited in Durgesh Rai, 'Patterns and Structure of the

Indian IT Industry: Scope for Strengthening India–Taiwan Ties', in *Proceedings of Advancing Regional Economic Integration: Potential Roles of India and Taiwan*, 25th Pacific Economic Community Seminar, 2 December 2010, Chinese Taipei Pacific Economic Cooperation Committee: 61–2.

34. See *The Impact of the IT–BPO Industry: A Decade in Review* (New Delhi: NASSCOM, 2010): 7.
35. See *Information Technology Annual Report 2005–06* (New Delhi: Ministry of Communications and Information Technology, 2006): 6.
36. Sen made these claims in his keynote speech at the 2007 NASSCOM India Leadership Summit. Sen has been the most balanced of all left-of-centre Indian intellectuals in his analysis of the software industry.
37. The figure of 30 per cent was cited in the *Information Technology Annual Report 2010–11* (New Delhi: Ministry of Communications and Information Technology, 2011): 2.
38. See C.P. Chandrasekhar and Jayati Ghosh, 'IT-driven Offshoring: The Exaggerated "Developmental Opportunity"', *Macroscan*, 2006, available at www.macroscan.com (last accessed 19 July 2011).
39. Microsoft also has influence in India via its founder, Bill Gates. During the 1990s Bill Gates was considered one of three 'Bills' which middle-class Indians tended to worship (the others being Bill Clinton and the dollar bill).
40. Rai, 'Patterns and Structure': 58.
41. Miria Pigato, *Information and Communication Technology, Poverty and Development in Sub-Saharan Africa and South Asia* (Washington, D.C.: World Bank, 2001): 57.
42. World Bank's 2008 Knowledge Economy Index (KEI), available at www.siteresources.worldbank.org (last accessed 19 July 2011).

CHAPTER 1

1. George Orwell, *Why I Write* (London: Penguin, 2004): 14.
2. John Maynard Keynes, 'Alfred Marshall 1842–1924', in J.M. Keynes (ed.), *Essays in Biography* (London: Palgrave Macmillan, 2010).
3. Non-resident Indian economists, such as Ashish Arora and V.N. Balasubramanyam, have been particularly prominent in advancing a neo-liberal portrayal.
4. The most influential work advocating this interpretation is Peter Evans's *Embedded Autonomy: States and Industrial Transformation* (Princeton, N.J.: Princeton University Press, 1985). A similar interpretation has come from Vibha Pingle in *Rethinking the Developmental State: India's Industry in Comparative Perspective* (New York: St Martin's Press, 1999).
5. See Thomas Friedman's articles in the *New York Times* for numerous references to the Indian software industry.
6. See Jay Lakhani, Hindu Tutor at Eton College and ubiquitous presence on the television channel Aastha TV, for an erudite explanation of such views.
7. Professors C.P. Chandraskehar and Jayati Ghosh noted that analyses of the Indian software industry do not distinguish between outsourcing and offshoring. See C.P. Chandrasekhar and Jayati Ghosh, 'IT-driven Offshoring: The Exaggerated Developmental Opportunity', *Macroscan*, 2006, available at www.macroscan.com (last accessed 19 July 2011).

CHAPTER 2

1. Cited in Anthony D'Costa, 'Uneven and Combined Development: Understanding India's Software Exports', *World Development* 31(1), 2003: 211.
2. Anthony D'Costa, 'The Indian Software Industry in the Global Division of Labour', in A. D'Costa and E. Sridharan (eds), *India in the Global Software Industry: Innovation, Firm Strategies and Development* (Basingstoke: Palgrave MacMillan, 2004): 11.
3. Ibid.
4. With the exception of BPO in front-desk operations.
5. This forced name change proved to be fortuitous: just a few years later Arthur Anderson became embroiled in the Enron scandal which, ultimately, led to the demise of the firm.
6. There is some debate over why IBM did this. Many consider that the US government's anti-monopoly regulation enforced the separation of hardware production and software provision. This explanation sits uneasily with the close relationship IBM and the US government enjoyed at the time (and, arguably, continue to do so to this very day). An alternative interpretation is that the separation of software and hardware provision provided a new lucrative market in the IT industry, which IBM could successfully exploit.
7. This was particularly the case in the provision of front-desk operations such as call centres, where only domestic telecommunications links could be relied upon with any certainty.
8. According to Professor Sumantra Ghoshal of the London Business School, what looked like global competition in the lower end of the software services industry in the 1990s was actually local competition between the three Indian Majors; cited in 'Indian Companies Need to Build Human Capital: Ghoshal', *Rediff*, 19 February 2001, available at www.rediff.com (last accessed 19 July 2011).
9. A large number of Indian BPO firms were bought by the Giants between 2004 and 2006. IBM set the tone with its acquisition of India's largest standalone BPO firm, Daksh. Other Giants then followed; for example, Cap Gemini acquired Indian BPO firm Indigo soon afterwards.

CHAPTER 3

1. In *The Economist*, 'The Remote Future', 19 February 2004.
2. In Gunnar Myrdal, *The Challenge of World Poverty* (London: Allen Lane, 1970): 3.
3. Polish philosopher Leszek Kolakowski has argued that any number of credible if not actual explanations can be put forward to explain any phenomenon, referring to this as the law of infinite cornucopia.
4. Friedman, *The World Is Flat: A Brief History of the Twenty-First Century* (London: Allen Lane, 2005): 4.
5. Ibid.: 5.
6. From www.sourcingmag.com (last accessed 19 July 2011). This is one of the most popular sites for practical advice to Western firms on outsourcing and offshoring.

7. US scholars have tended not to assign any role for the English language in the development of the Indian software industry. British scholars, in contrast, have continuously emphasised its importance. This could be coincidence. However, it might also be a result of what the novelist Salman Rushdie observed as a predilection in Britain to look back fondly on the Raj and attribute any positive developments in South Asia to its imperial policies. See Salman Rushdie, *Imaginary Homelands* (London: Granta Books, 1992): 130. Dr Sumita Mukherjee, in her doctoral thesis *The Experience of the 'England-Returned': The Education of Indians in Britain in the Early Twentieth Century and Its Long-Term Impact* (D.Phil. dissertation, Oxford University, 2008), takes this predilection to its extreme, arguing that India's eventual independence from the United Kingdom was primarily a result of the access of a small minority of Indians to the British higher education system, in particular the Oxbridge colleges. Adopting this line of argument offers an intriguing counterfactual – had Nehru, Gandhi and Subhas Chandra Bose not been educated in the United Kingdom, would India still be the jewel in the British crown? Surely even the greatest admirers of the Raj would struggle to concur.

8. See the *Financial Times Survey of the World's Most Respected Companies* (London: PWC Publications, 2004): 18. The survey lists the 200 leading global companies. Of the nine IT firms which made it into the list, seven were from the United States (HP, IBM, Dell, Microsoft, Cisco, Intel, Oracle), one was from Germany (SAP) and one was from India (Infosys).

9. Thomas Friedman, 'The Great Indian Dream', *New York Times*, 11 March 2004.

10. Cheryll Barron, 'The Indian Genius: What Makes Indian Software Developers the Best in the World', *Prospect* 97, 2004.

11. Their absence in Confucian tradition, where independent thought, creativity, and speculation are suppressed in favour of obedience to authority and a fixation of the practical code of living and governing, has also been used to explain the glaring failure of the software industry in Japan (and by extension other countries with a Confucian heritage) to become internationally competitive. See Setsuo Ohsuga, 'Barriers to Software Development in Japan', *Computing Japan* 5(3), 1998 for an intriguing take on how Japanese culture has impeded the country's ability to compete in the global software industry. Ohsuga argues that Japanese collectivism, in contrast to Western individualism, is the key impediment.

12. There has been much talk about the role of the Indian Institutes of Technology (IITs) in the development of the Indian software industry. However, alumni of these most prestigious of technical institutes are better represented in US IT firms than in Indian ones. For example, while only Infosys and Patni Computer Systems were founded by IIT alumni, US IT giants such as Sun Microsystems, CISCO and Novell were all either founded by IIT alumni or have had a CEO from an IIT. And yet no one would argue that the US IT industry developed as a result of the IITs – that would be deemed ridiculous. It is therefore equally banal to attribute the development of the Indian software industry to them.

13. See Chris Fuller and Hari Narasimhan, 'From Landlords to Software Engineers: Migration and Urbanisation Amongst Tamil Brahmins', *Comparative Studies in Society and History* 50, 2008:170, where culture is used to explain the caste profile of the Indian software industry's labour force. According to the two

scholars, the over-representation of Brahmins in the software industry is seen to reflect 'their caste tradition of learning'.

14. See Priyamvada Gopal, 'India: A Portrait by Patrick French – A Review', *Guardian*, 5 February 2011.

15. Balaji Parthsarthy, 'Globalizing Information Technology: The Domestic Policy Context for India's Software Production and Exports', *Iterations: The Interdisciplinary Journal of Software History* 3, 2004.

16. Cited from Steve Hamm's 'Visa Abuse? Help from India', *Business Week*, 18 May 2009, available at www.businessweek.com (last accessed 19 July 2011).

17. The firm in question was PixL Software Service Solutions. While the explicit bias within PixL's job advertisement was rare, it confirmed to many American-born IT workers what they had already felt for some years: that American IT firms preferred Indian software programmers over American-born ones.

18. The Arabs, conveyors of Vedic mathematics to Europe, referred to mathematics as 'Hindsat', the science of the Hindus.

19. Many such works exist examining the differing 'performances' amongst various ethnic communities. For the most succinct yet detailed piece of analysis I have come across, see Lucinda Platt, *Migration and Social Mobility: The Life Chances of Britain's Minority Ethnic Communities* (London: Policy Press, 2005). Indians were found to do better than all other ethnic groups in all indicators of educational achievement. In a fillip to the 'innate Indic ability' line of thought, Platt disaggregated Indians in Britain by religion, finding that of all religious groups of Indian origin, Hindus enjoyed the highest levels of achievement.

20. V.N. and A. Balasubramanyam, 'The Software Cluster in Bangalore', in John Dunning (ed.), *Regions, Globalization and the Knowledge-Based Economy* (Oxford: Oxford University Press, 2000): 361.

21. See Athreye, 'The Indian Software Industry', in Ashish Arora and Alain Gambardella (eds), *From Underdogs to Tigers: The Rise and Growth of the Software Industry in Brazil, China, India, Ireland and Israel* (Oxford: Oxford University Press, 2005).

22. CAGR for software exports in the 1970s (1975–78) and 1980s (1981–85) calculated from DoE data cited by Vibha Pingle in *Rethinking the Developmental State: India's Industry in Comparative Perspective* (New York: St Martin's Press, 1999): 121. CAGR for 1998–2008 calculated from NASSCOM Annual Reports.

23. Arora and Gambardella, *From Underdogs to Tigers*: 2.

24. Balasubramanyam and Balasubramanyam, 'The Software Cluster in Bangalore': 361.

25. See Meredith Woo-Cummings (ed.), *The Developmental State* (London: Cornell University Press, 1999) for a good, if basic, introduction to the major theoretical debates within, and empirical examples of, the Developmental State Paradigm.

26. See Mushtaq Khan's *Rents, Rent-seeking and Economic Development: Theory and the Asian Evidence* (Cambridge: Cambridge University Press, 2000) for a counterintuitive argument which posits that corruption and clientelism need not be a fetter on economic development and can, under certain circumstances, facilitate it.

27. For the seminal work on the hold of special interest groups over the Indian state, see Pranab Bardhan's *The Political Economy of India* (Oxford: Blackwell, 1984).

28. Balaji Parthsarthy, 'Globalizing Information Technology: The Domestic Policy Context for India's Software Production and Exports', *Iterations: The Inter-disciplinary Journal of Software History* 3, 2004.

29. Murali Patibandla and Bent Pederson, 'The Role of Transnational Corporations in the Evolution of a High-Tech Industry: The Case of India's Software Industry', *World Development* 30, 2002.

30. Firm lobbying in India has tended to be individualistic rather than collective. This is a result of the firms' interests, which were to secure government contracts or licences. However, software firms were not interested in securing individual licences or government contracts but in the state's provision of collective products such as advanced telecommunications infrastructure. See Chapter 7 for an evaluation of NASSCOM's ability in the late 1980s to lobby the Indian state.

31. For example, India's Business Houses have always had an interest in ensuring access to cheap computers and would, therefore, oppose moves to raise tariffs as part of an infant computer industry strategy. The considerable influence of Business Houses cannot, then, be overlooked when considering how and for whom IT policy is constructed.

32. The subversion of one major IT policy by vested interests has been discussed in detail in by C.R. Subramanium in his excellent book *India and the Computer: A Study in Planned Development* (New Delhi: Oxford University Press, 1992). While this book was cited in the bibliographies of the two major pieces of work from the Developmental Department literature – Peter Evans's *Embedded Autonomy: States and Industrial Transformation* (Princeton, N.J.: Princeton University Press, 1985) and Vibha Pingle's *Rethinking the Developmental State: India's Industry in Comparative Perspective* (New York: St Martin's Press, 1999) – both chose to overlook his substantive analysis.

33. Evans, *Embedded Autonomy*: 99.

34. Ohsuga, 'Barriers to Software Development in Japan'.

35. Cited in 'The IT Indians: A Tribute to the People Who Have Helped Turn the Indian IT Dream into Reality', in Dataquest, 2002 available at http://dqindia.ciol.com (last accessed 19 July 2011).

36. See Paul Herbig, *Innovation Japanese Style: A Cultural and Historical Perspective* (Westport, Conn.: Quorum, 1995): 10; and Daniel Breznit, 'Development, Flexibility and R&D Performance in the Taiwanese IT Industry: Capability Creation and the Effects of State–Industry Co-evolution', *Industrial and Corporate Change* 14, 2005: 153–87.

37. The importance of the character of the computer hardware installed based in India for the development of the country's software industry will be amply illustrated in Chapter 6.

CHAPTER 4

1. In Karl Marx and Friedrich Engels, *The Communist Manifesto* (London: Longman, 2005): 219.

2. See Chapter 6 in Evans, *Embedded Autonomy: States and Industrial Transformation* (Princeton, N.J.: Princeton University Press, 1985).

3. For example, the change in leadership within the DoE was part of a wider change in the Indian state directly reflecting the election of the Janata Party

to power and the return to political influence of India's Business Houses; see Chapter 6.

4. Even more nuanced works from a similar perspective, such as Vibha Pingle's *Rethinking the Developmental State: India's Industry in Comparative Perspective* (New York: St Martin's Press, 1999) while acknowledging the presence of IT capital and its interaction with the state, still perceive the state as autonomous. The result is a simplistic account of IT capital as a consultant, aiding the DoE in fine-tuning policy. Policy formulation is presented as unwaveringly anodyne: at no point does Pingle acknowledge the possibility that the interventions drawn up by the state might reflect narrow vested interests rather than the greater good of the industry.

5. The Cambridge economist Ha-Joon Chang's book *Kicking Away the Ladder: Development Policy in Historical Perspective* (London: Anthem, 2003) illustrates in great detail the integral role of state intervention in the industrialisation of all currently developed countries, including those alleged bastions of the free market, the USA and the United Kingdom. These states were far from insulated from societal pressures during their periods of rapid industrialisation.

6. This will be explored in Part 3.

7. See Kwon-Hee Lee, 'Industrial Policy and Industrialisation in South Korea: The Case of the Car Industry', in Ben Fine, Jyoti Saraswati and Daniela Tavasci (eds), *Beyond the Developmental State: Industrial Policy into the Twenty-First Century* (London: Pluto Press, 2012).

8. For an understanding of the exponential growth of the software industry, see Richard Heeks, *The Indian Software Industry: State Policy, Liberalisation and Industrial Development* (New Delhi: Sage, 1996): 109.

9. Pingle's *Rethinking the Developmental State* argued that the superior performance of the software industry vis-à-vis the steel industry in India was primarily related to the differences in the government departments or ministries responsible for the sectors. However, this viewpoint overlooks the differences in growth of their respective markets, as pointed out by Simon Commander in 'What Explains the Growth of the Software Industry in Some Emerging Markets', in S. Commander (ed.), *The Software Industry in Emerging Markets* (Cheltenham: Edward Elgar, 2005): 17.

10. See Pingle, *Rethinking the Developmental State*: 136.

11. Evans, *Embedded Autonomy*: 168.

12. Pingle, *Rethinking the Developmental State*: 135.

13. See Joseph Grieco, *Between Dependence and Autonomy: India's Experiences with the International Computer Industry* (Berkeley: University of California Press, 1984) for an early misreading of the Minicomputer Policy.

14. The interpretation of the Minicomputer Policy as facilitating an illicit trading regime comes from an industry insider – C.R. Subramanium – in *India and the Computer*.

CHAPTER 5

1. Cited in N. Rajadhyaksha, *The Rise of India: Its Transformation from Poverty to Prosperity* (Singapore: Wiley and Son, 2007): 1.

2. See Chapter 8 of R. Palme-Dutt, *The Crisis of Britain and the British Empire* (London: Lawrence and Wishart, 1953) for a description of how Western powers maintained control of their former colonies despite – or perhaps thanks

to – formal independence. The primary rationale was economic, in particular to maintain the economically exploitative relations that had developed during the colonial period.

3. Herbert Humphrey, the US vice-president during the Johnson administration, is widely credited as the architect of the 'food as a lever' strategy in US foreign policy.

4. The reasons for India's problems in producing enough food for the population are manifold. One of the chief reasons, however, was the Land Tax imposed under British rule. This shifted land usage in India from food production towards cash crop cultivation, increasing the vulnerability of large sections of the population to food shortages or hikes in the price of foodstuffs. For a fuller examination into the role of the land tax, see Isaiah Bowman, *The New World: Problems in Human Geography* (New York: Nabu Press, 2010).

5. See Sumit Ganguly, 'Of Great Expectations and Bitter Disappointments: Indo-US Relations under the Johnson Administration', *Asian Affairs* 15(4), 1988: 217–18 for a description of the US utilisation of its food lever in relation to Indian government criticism of the US role in Vietnam.

6. From Narendra Singh Sarila, *In the Shadow of the Great Game: The Untold Story of India's Partition* (London: Constable, 2007).

7. V.L. Kelkar, 'India and the World Economy: the Search for Self-Reliance', *Economic and Political Weekly*, Annual Number, February 1980: 249.

8. Stephen Cohen and Richard Park, *India: Emergent Power?* (New York: Crane, Russak and Co., 1978).

9. See Bhiku Parek, 'The Marxist Discourse on Gandhi', in Deepa Tripathi (ed.), *Business and Politics in India: A Historical Perspective* (New Delhi: Manohar, 1991): 198 for an acknowledgement that Gandhi's economic thought was 'strange, self-contradictory and not easy to classify'.

10. The Bombay Plan – an industrial policy drawn up by the patriarchs of the seven leading Business Houses in 1944 – provided an indication as to what India's corporatist model might look like once independence was achieved.

11. Far from being rivals, the Business Houses and foreign corporations had amicable, even close relations.

12. The intermediate class is discussed at length in Prem Shankhar Jha's *The Political Economy of Stagnation* (Bombay: Oxford University Press, 1980).

13. The intermediate class pushed through the Monopolies and Restrictive Trading Policies (MRTP), which took the reservation system to a whole new level in 1969. This was without doubt their 'greatest' political feat.

14. Moraji Desai had a well-earned reputation as a close friend of the Business Houses. This reputation became particularly pronounced after he famously took issue with the Indian Government's *Hazari Committee Report* (1967), which accused the Business Houses (and in particular the Birlas) of corruption. For more details on Indira Gandhi's political intrigues and machinations, see Pupul Jayakar's *Indira Gandhi: A Biography* (New Delhi: Viking, 1992).

15. The first official government enquiry into the role of information technology in India was the *Bhabha Report* (1966). The report was named after the nuclear scientist Homi Bhabha, who chaired the enquiry. The report recommended the promotion of wholly owned Indian computer firms to satisfy the bulk of India's computer requirements. It also advocated the dilution of foreign computer firm subsidiaries operating in India in order that such subsidiaries could be run in a manner conducive to India's computerisation agenda.

16. Vibha Pingle, *Rethinking the Developmental State: India's Industry in Comparative Perspective* (New York: St Martin's Press, 1999): 123.

17. Cited in C.R. Subramanium, *India and the Computer: A Study in Planned Development* (New Delhi: Oxford University Press, 1992): 76.

18. As the term suggests, this involves the state protecting and nurturing the company in its early stages until it becomes able to compete in a free market without government support. This was far from a maverick strategy adopted by novice Indian bureaucrats in a sunrise industry – it had been successfully applied across a number of sectors in Germany, the United States and Japan as well as in many other countries over the previous two centuries. For the seminal work on the history of infant-industry protection, see Ha-Joon Chang, *Kicking Away the Ladder: Development Policy in Historical Perspective* (London: Anthem, 2002).

19. For an excellent explanation of this situation, see Pingle, *Rethinking the Developmental State*: 124.

20. John Maisonrouge was speaking in his official capacity as president of IBM at the Hearings Before the Group of Eminent Persons to Study the Impact of Multinational Corporations on Development and on International Relations, United Nations, New York. He was joined by Gary Johns, the chairman of the board. A fuller exposition of this issue is presented in A.Z. Astapovich, *The Strategy of Transnational Corporations* (Moscow: Progress Publishers, 1978): 121.

21. Professor Astapovich, writing in the 1970s, noted that other major US companies, such as General Motors, Honeywell, and Motorola, were similarly concerned with ensuring full control of all their subsidiaries – Astapovich, *The Strategy of Transnational Corporations*: 121. That these firms are all engaged in higher-end production involving advanced technology suggests that factors other than managerial problems – such as national security concerns – have dictated their desire for maintaining full control.

22. The Indian government, in bargaining with IBM to help computerise the country in return for access to the market, was not some anomalous outlier country. The Japanese government made similar demands. However, negotiations between the Japanese state and IBM took on a very different hue from negotiations between IBM and India. The result was that IBM retained full control of its Japanese subsidiary but was forced to comply with the Japanese state's various other requirements. For example, IBM was forced to export a certain percentage of the computers it produced in Japan, release patents to Japanese companies at reduced royalty rates, and to develop local component suppliers. Moreover, it was only allowed to sell certain types of computers in the Japanese market; other segments of the computer market were reserved for Japanese companies. See J. Dedrick and K.L. Kraemer, *Asia's Computer Challenge: Threat or Opportunity for the United States and the World* (New York: Oxford University Press): 42–6 for a more detailed account of the requirements with which IBM was forced to comply. It is not known why IBM's negotiations with Japan has such a different outcome from its negotiations with India, but this is probably due to a combination of three possible explanations. First, the Japanese state was a better negotiator than the Indian state. They could therefore wrangle better concessions than the Indian state, or were less dogmatic in their requirement of dilution. Second, there might be an economic rationale – for example, perhaps the IBM management felt that the Japanese market offered far better mid-term

returns to IBM than the Indian market, and hence maintaining a presence was a requirement. Third, there may well have been a geopolitical dimension. Japan was (and for the most part still is) a subordinate ally of the USA. In contrast, India professed to be socialist and, following the 1971 Indo-Pakistani war, had been far closer to the USSR than to the USA. President Richard Nixon and his advisor Henry Kissinger regularly referred to the Indian prime minister Indira Gandhi as 'the bitch' and despised the Indian government for what they saw as a lack of deference to American power. It is highly conceivable that IBM consulted the US government over its global investment policy and was advised to 'play hardball' with the Indians. If geopolitics was a reason, to see just how far the Indo-US relationship has developed, consider the recent Indo-US nuclear deal. General Electric has played a major role in lobbying for the deal – unsurprisingly, in view of the huge profits the deal ensures. But what is interesting is just how relaxed the US government has been about the deal, despite the fact that it blatantly undermines the USA's stated position for over half a century on issues relating to the proliferation of nuclear technology.

23. The name ICL was gradually phased out after the firm was acquired by the Japanese electronics firm Fujitsu in 1990.

24. Grieco, *Between Dependence and Autonomy: India's Experiences with the International Computer Industry* (Berkeley: University of California Press, 1984): 286.

25. More precisely, there were 111 computers in India in 1970 – see Subramanium, *India and the Computer*: 6.

26. Grieco, *Between Dependence and Autonomy*: 207.

27. For a discussion on how the Indian state in the 1970s somehow conflated self-reliance (making everything) and self-sufficiency (having the ability to make everything if necessary), see Amiya Bagchi's 'Technological Self-reliance in Dependence and Underdevelopment', in A. Wad (ed.) *Science, Technology and Development* (Boulder, Colo.: Westview Press, 1988). Bagchi makes the case that India's obsession with self-reliance rather than self-sufficiency impeded technological development by allowing the country to get bogged down in pure research.

28. Grieco, *Between Dependence and Autonomy*: 240.

29. Pingle, *Rethinking the Developmental State*: 128.

30. Subramanium, *India and the Computer*: 27.

31. For more information on this period see *TCS: The Pioneer of the Indian IT Industry* (New Delhi: ICMR Case Studies Collection, 2004).

32. While the name Burroughs is no longer a name one would associate with computers, at the time it was one of the leading computer manufacturers and a ubiquitous presence on the global IT landscape. Since the mid 1980s it has gone through so many mergers and acquisitions that the name was eventually phased out of existence. Equally interesting is that the relationship between Tata and Burroughs was a result of IBM's removal from the Indian market.

33. Cited in S. Mahalingham, 'From the President's Desk', *Computer Society of India*, 1 April 2009.

34. From *TCS: The Pioneer of the Indian IT Industry*.

35. Following its contract with the Central Bank of India, within the next two years, TCS won contracts to write similar systems for 14 other Indian banks. These skills were integral to its winning the contract in 1974 to provide software

services to the Institutional Group and Data Company (IGDC), a data centre for ten US banks. For more information, see ibid.

36. Balaji Parthsarthy, 'Globalizing Information Technology: The Domestic Policy Context for India's Software Production and Exports', *Iterations: The Interdisciplinary Journal of Software History* 3, 2004.

37. While a nascent software services industry was already present in India, it is inconceivable that without the Software Export Scheme this industry would have started to export its services. Even in the West, software services provision in one country was primarily carried out by firms from the same country. For example, Hoskyns would provide software services in the UK and Cap Gemini in France. Even the industry leader, the US firm EDS, lacked an international focus. Unlikely as it may seem, India therefore led the world in cross-border software services provision (even if the quality of the services provided by Indian firms was relatively basic vis-à-vis Western software services providers and most of the service was carried out onsite).

38. Subramanium, *India and the Computer*: 185.

CHAPTER 6

1. In 'Unintended Consequences', Library of Economics and Liberty, available at www.econlib.org/index.html (last accessed 19 July 2011).

2. The words of the respected independence movement leader Jayaprakash Narayan who, like many others, perceived the Emergency to be an outcome of Indira Gandhi's own thirst for power.

3. Lloyd Rudolph and Susan Rudolph, *In Pursuit of Lakshmi: The Political Economy of the Indian State* (New Delhi: Orient Longman, 1987): 232.

4. Hence there was little surprise when an Indian industrialist, interviewed in the months before the 1977 election, boasted that corruption in the USA was 'chickenfeed compared to what Business Houses were giving the Congress Party'; cited in Michael Henderson, *Experiment with Untruth: India Under Emergency* (New Delhi: Macmillan, 1977): 169.

5. The Janata Party primarily comprised three large independent parties – Bharatiya Lok Dal, Bharatiya Jana Sangh, Socialist Party – plus the party of Congress dissenters (Congress (O)) and a range of small parties. The Janata Party was often referred to as the 'Grand Alliance', reflecting its broad constituency.

6. One of the key themes in V.S. Naipaul's *India: A Million Mutinies Now* (London, Heinemann, 1990) was the Emergency's role in facilitating the criminalisation of business and politics in India.

7. The Janata Party's election manifesto can be found in the appendices of V.K. Narasimhan's *Democracy Redeemed* (New Delhi: Sage, 1977). Of the 13 points in the manifesto's Economic Charter, Point 3 justifies the decentralisation of the economy on the grounds that it is a Gandhian approach, while Point 5 evokes the importance of technology for self-reliance.

8. Janata and Congress shared the view that small, fully open markets were often plagued by overcapacity, price wars, scarcity of resources, etc. However, rather than this requiring the direct role of the state as producer, Janata eulogised the East Asian tigers and their practice of controlled private-sector competition. Controlled competition, whereby a select few firms are allowed to enter sectors, was seen to be superior to monopoly due to inclusion of a competitive element.

As such, the Janata Party made a play that they would replace state monopolies with controlled competition using the standard practice of licensing.

9. According to his sympathetic biographer, G.S. Bhargava, Desai's 'antipathy to socialists was total'; see G.S. Bhargava, *Moraji Desai, Prime Minister of India* (New Delhi: India Books Co., 1977). This probably explains why Desai was courted by London and Washington as 'their man'. It could be safely assumed that a man of such 'calibre' would be unlikely to lead the country to a Gandhian socialist revolution.

10. Take, for example, Janata's rationale for breaking state monopolies and introducing controlled competition via a licensing system. The Janata leadership proclaimed this system as empowering small firms to become large firms and to challenge the concentration of the Business Houses. It did exactly the opposite, however. Rather than empowering new firms, the system was rigged in favour of the established Business Houses; those with the connections, finance and savoir-faire would get the licences they wanted. Those outside such circles, in contrast, were barred from entry. Moreover, the Business Houses could flout the conditions of the licences without any fear that the state would reprimand them, let alone revoke their licences. Some firms openly produced in excess of licensed quotas. Others would buy up all the production licences for a sector to prevent entry by competitors. As early as 1979 the Committee on Controls and Subsidies had conceded that the licensing system had ceased to be an instrument in fostering development; cited in Sudip Chaudhuri, 'Industrialisation', ín Terry Byres (ed.), *The Indian Economy: Major Debates Since Independence* (New Delhi: Oxford University Press, 1998): 275. An even more damning evaluation of the open and unpunished abuse of the licensing system by the Indian private sector was published in 1983 by the Corporate Studies Group – see *Economic and Political Weekly*, 30 April 1983, for the full findings.

11. See Trevor Drieberg and S.J. Mohan, *Emergency in India* (New Delhi: Manas Publishing, 1975) for an account of the Emergency which identifies the opposition to Indira Gandhi's rule (including prominent members of the Janata Party) as being the proxies of Western agents.

12. Niccolo Machiavelli (1467–1527), the Florentine Renaissance diplomat, was renowned for the theorisation of effective, if ruthless and amoral, statecraft. Max Weber, the nineteenth-century German sociologist, was famed for his work on the state and the efficiency of bureaucracy.

13. Menon had been a scientist at the Tata Institute for Fundamental Research, traditionally close to the Department of Atomic Energy under whose jurisdiction ECIL operated.

14. Homi J. Bhabha – one of the strongest advocates of Indian self-sufficiency and inspiration behind many of the DoE's early policies – was a scientific giant in India. He was however much more than an excellent scientist. He was also a fierce believer in national sovereignty.

15. Balaji Parthsarthy, 'Globalizing Information Technology: The Domestic Policy Context for India's Software Production and Exports', *Iterations: The Interdisciplinary Journal of Software History* 3, 2004.

16. Ibid.

17. In 1977, prior to his transfer, Professor Menon had lined up a number of calculator firms to enter the computer components and peripherals production process. The Minicomputer Report claimed that it would be following up on this.

18. C.R. Subramanium, *India and the Computer: A Study in Planned Development* (New Delhi: Oxford University Press, 1992).

19. Even if the DoE was only half-committed to developing a computer industry in India, it might at least have used the period of protection to enforce R&D-based competitive production for the better-managed Indian computer companies. It did not even do this – see C.P. Chandrasekhar, 'The Diffusion of Information Technology and the Implications for Global Development: A Perspective Based on the Indian Experience', *Macroscan* 2003: 20–1, available at www.macroscan. com (last accessed 19 July 2011).

20. Subramanium, *India and the Computer*: 185.

21. J. Dedrick and K.L. Kraemer, *Asia's Computer Challenge: Threat or Opportunity for the United States and the World* (New York: Oxford University Press, 1998): 42–6.

22. The differentiation between larger and smaller Indian computer hardware firms was less pronounced than might be thought. Production differences were not of great significance; however, the larger firms provided a reliable after-sales service and thereby gained a better reputation.

23. With no commitment, what was to stop the government from liberalising computer imports before international competitiveness was achieved? And if it did, then the reinvested profits would have gone to waste, as the firms would have been unable to compete with their foreign competitors. Better, therefore, to enjoy the profits as they were generated or reinvest them in other, safer lines of business.

24. They could remain competitive vis-à-vis the larger firms by smuggling in the knock-down kits from abroad and hence evading customs duties. According to C.P. Chandrasekhar, these firms were satisfied with their extremely low profit margins; see Chandrasekhar, 'The Diffusion of Information Technology': 20.

25. Ibid.: 24.

26. Jessican Ma, a specialist on IT, notes how the presence of bundling stifled the emergence of the Chinese software industry. According to Ma, 'the [Chinese] customers want software integrated with their product. This makes it very hard to sell stand-alone software. The large [computer] companies in China prefer to develop their own software'; cited in Anna Lee Saxenian, 'Government and Guanxi: The Chinese Software Industry in Transition', a paper presented at the Global Software from Emerging Markets conference, London Business School, 12 May 2003. Similarly, Professor Anthony D'Costa argues that the practice of bundling has inhibited the emergence of a Japanese software industry. Writing in a research paper for the World Bank, he notes that 'highly competitive Japanese [computer] hardware producers have always bundled their software, hence the development of an independent software industry in Japan has been discouraged'. See *Exports, University–Industry Linkages and Innovation Challenges in Bangalore, India* (Washington, D.C.: World Bank, 2006): 20. For more information on the lack of a Japanese software industry, see M. Anchordoguy, 'Japan's Software Industry: A Failure of Institutions?', *Research Policy* 29(3), 2000: 391–408.

27. Professor C.P. Chandrasekhar is one of the few academics to have not only examined both the Indian computer hardware industry and the software industry but to have examined the relationship between the two. See Chandrasekhar, 'The Diffusion of Information Technology': 20.

28. Using data from Vibha Pingle, *Rethinking the Developmental State: India's Industry in Comparative Perspective* (New York: St Martin's Press, 1999): 121.

CHAPTER 7

1. In an interview with Jeremy Paxman on the BBC's *Newsnight*, a daily television news programme, 2 June 2011 .
2. C.P. Chandrasekhar and Jayati Ghosh, *The Market That Failed: a Decade of Neo-liberal Economic Reforms in India* (New Delhi: Leftword, 2002): 6.
3. This desire amongst a developing country's middle classes is by no means unique to India. However, such a desire was particularly pronounced in India due to what is known as the NRI (non-resident Indian) effect. The NRI effect is the notion that NRIs have played an important role in transmitting the consumerism prevalent in the West to their relatives in India, in part through back-migration and remittances.
4. In order to achieve desirable scale, Business Houses were encouraged to enter sectors previously reserved for smaller-scale production.
5. This is taking a short-termist perspective. A longer-term horizon would focus on engendering an indigenous R&D base. However, a democratic framework generally promotes short-termism.
6. The PC was made possible by three technological changes that occurred in the 1970s. First was the improvement of price/performance ratios for semiconductors. Second was modularity, whereby components came to be standardised, allowing for their sourcing in the open market. And finally there was the movement away from closed to open systems, which allowed switching between systems.
7. As the OECD noted, 'the digital revolution had helped [in theory] to overcome the problem [of body-shopping]'; see OECD's *Information Technology Outlook* (Paris: OECD, 2010): 7.
8. It is necessary to realise that the state's need to sustain the pattern of accumulation via exports was a precondition for the pro-software intervention. Without this, it would not have made the huge outlays on physical telecommunications infrastructure. However, there were two further factors supporting the state's pro-software export interventions more generally in the late 1980s and 1990s. First, there was Dewang Mehta, NASSCOM's first executive director. He was 'a shrewd lobbyist' and 'irrepressible cheerleader' for the industry, according to Cheryl Bentsen; see 'Dewang Mehta in the Middle', *CIO*, 1 December 2000. For more information on Dewang Mehta, also see Vinita Chawla's edited volume, *Dewang Mehta: Collected Thoughts* (New Delhi: NASSCOM, 2002). Second, the software industry was better able to mobilise its firms and organise them effectively than other associations. This was primarily due to most of the firms' founders coming from the same strata of society, with matching educational profiles and socialising in overlapping circles of family and friends. However, both factors are more relevant to the fine-tuning of policy after the provision of infrastructure rather than in initiating it. NASSCOM had only been created and Mehta appointed executive director after the decision had been made to build the appropriate infrastructure.
9. DDL enthusiasts have claimed that the infrastructure provision was due to Pranab Sen, the DoE's economic advisor. The rationale is poor – Sen was apparently 'the first to note that the lack of data communication facilities meant

India was unable to take advantage of the global demand for data-entry services';
see Balaji Parthsarthy, 'Globalizing Information Technology: The Domestic
Policy Context for India's Software Production and Exports', *Iterations: The
Interdisciplinary Journal of Software History* 3, 2004. But whether or not Sen
was the first to identify the opportunity and the impediments is beside the point.
It certainly does not automatically mean that the state would invest tens of
millions of dollars in the provision of data communication facilities. Only the
wider political economy context can explain why the state acted in the way it
did. This argument proffered by Parthsarthy again shows the problems inherent
within the DDL literature.

10. One example is the state's heavily subsidised trip for Indian software firms to
the CeBIT (Centrum fur Buroatomation Informationstechnologie und Telekom-
minikation) event in Hanover in 1989. CeBIT was and is the world's largest
trade show in IT and telecommunications. In addition to displaying various
new innovations in IT, it was also a hotbed of networking between buyers and
sellers across the industry.

11. However, while notable, these interventions were not novel, but were mere
extensions to the various policies attached to and in place since the 1972
Software Export Scheme. For a monumental 3,000-word description of these
IT policy changes in the late 1980s, see Parthsarthy, 'Globalizing Information
Technology'.

12. While it was open to both computer hardware and software firms, the primary
intention of MAIT had been to give computer manufacturing firms 'a coherent
voice in the corridors of power'; see E. Sridharan, *The Political Economy of
Industrial Promotion* (London: Praegar, 1996): 180.

13. This defensive and ultimately futile struggle has been well documented in Pingle,
Rethinking the Developmental State: 144.

14. Gubir Singh, 'IT is a Global Chartbuster', *Economic Times*, 16 October 2002.

15. Cited in Kanchana Suggu, 'Share of High-End IT Work Zooms', *Rediff*,
9 February 2001, available at www.rediff.com (last accessed 19 July 2011).

16. From Sujay Marthi's 'NASSCOM: The Face of the IT Industry', 8 December
2006, available at www.mouthshut.com (last accessed 19 July 2011). According
to legend, the decision to form NASSCOM was made in a Boston bar following
a software delegation to the USA. It has become known as the Boston Scotch
Party, though Boston IT Party would be a better term. See Shivanand Kanavi,
'The Story of NASSCOM', *Business India*, 19 February 2001, available at
http://reflections-shivanand.blogspot.com/2008/01/story-of-nasscom.html (last
accessed 19 July 2011).

17. Cited in Kanavi, 'The Story of NASSCOM'.

CHAPTER 8

1. Cited on the website of the National Alliance of Peoples Movement, available
at http://napm-india.org (last accessed 19 July 2011).

2. See Aditya Chakrabortty, 'Is this the Indian Century?', *Guardian*, 29 March
2008.

3. One of the leading proponents of this view is Kishore Mahbubani, former
Singaporean permanent representative to the UN and high-profile cheerleader
of the 'Asian Century' idea, in which China and India will, within the next
two decades, come to dominate the global political economy. See Kishore

Mahbubani, *The New Asian Hemisphere: The Irresistible Shift of Global Power to the East* (New York: Public Affairs, 2008).

4. Recent high-end non-fiction books describing the rise of India have all devoted ample space to its software industry. Examples include Edward Luce's *In Spite of the Gods: The Strange Rise of Modern India* (London: Anchor, 2008) and Patrick French's *India: A Portrait* (London: Random House, 2011).

5. These firms were, invariably, individual family- or caste-based medium-sized enterprises run by highly motivated founders. Their primary interest was in entering lucrative industrial sectors dominated by the Business Houses; liberalisation, in the form of the abolition of controls and the permitting of foreign collaboration, was their means to achieve such entry.

6. An exception was the case of K.V.K. Raju, who beat the Birlas to win a licence to build a fertiliser factory. Raju's company achieved this feat by entering into financial and technical collaboration with the Italian TNC Snamprogetti, which had direct access to then Prime Minister Indira Gandhi via her daughter-in-law, Sonia.

7. See C.P. Chandrasekhar and Jayati Ghosh, *The Market That Failed: a Decade of Neo-liberal Economic Reforms in India* (New Delhi: Leftword, 2002): 34.

8. For example, under the United Front Government in the 1990s, two key economic ministries – industry and commerce – were held by regionalist parties: Andhra Pradesh's DMK and Tamil Nadu's TDP respectively. See Sanjaya Baru, 'Economic Policy and the Development of Capitalism in India', in Francine Frankel, Zoya Hassan, Rajeev Bhargava and Balveer Arora (eds), *Transforming India: Social and Political Dynamics of Democracy* (New Delhi: Oxford University Press, 2002): 225.

9. Balveer Arora, 'Negotiating Differences: Federal Coalitions and National Cohesion', in Frankel et al., *Transforming India*: 181.

10. To enter export markets dominated by foreign capital in any meaningful way requires a quid pro quo – foreign capital would expect to have access to the domestic market. There was indeed a slackening of resistance to liberalisation as Business Houses started to enter the export markets; see Chandrasekhar and Ghosh, *The Market That Failed*: 32.

11. Partha Chatterjee, 'Democracy and Economic Transformation in India', *Economic and Political Weekly*, 19 April 2008: 56.

12. Cited ibid.: 57.

13. By the turn of the century most of the Indian middle classes had some family members based in the USA.

14. Relatedly, a Pew Poll carried out in 2005 found that Indians were the most pro-American of any of the 16 major countries polled; 71 per cent of Indians said they had a positive view of America, with just 55 per cent of British people concurring and 23 per cent of Pakistanis. See Pew Global Attitudes Survey, available at www.pewglobal.org/2005/06/23/us-image-up-slightly-but-still-negative (last accessed 28 September 2011).

15. See Biplab Dasgupta, *Globalization: India's Adjustment Experience* (New Delhi: Sage, 2005).

16. *The Economist* was one of the first Western media outlets to identify this. In 2004 it stated that 'the global professional-services giants such as IBM, Ernst and Young, and Accenture are taking on upstart competitors such as Wipro and Infosys'; *The Economist*, 'The Remote Future', 19 February 2004.

17. *The Economist* referred to such firms as 'full service providers, able to take on everything from writing software applications to managing the payroll'; *The Economist*, 'The Remote Future'.

18. Moreover, once one of the Giants began to emulate the Indian Majors, the other Giants were compelled to follow suit out of sheer competitive pressure. As the OECD reports, 'once the process [of offshoring] begins, competition drives all firms in an industry to adopt a similar strategy since cost-reducing organisational changes have this in common with technical change'; see OECD, *The Service Economy* (Paris: OECD, 2000): 7.

19. There are also the material interests of the Indian software firms to consider. For them, maintaining access to the US market was important. Having US TNCs in NASSCOM could significantly bolster their influence in the USA, with positive implications for their ability to stall any moves to increase protectionism in the US market.

20. The Executive Council, normally holding between 20 and 30 members, is responsible for the general management of NASSCOM. Broadly defined, this includes setting aims, objectives and strategies. See Appendices for the internal power structure of NASSCOM.

21. Thus, a firm (or subsidiary) with revenues exceeding Rs 500 crore would have six votes while a firm with Rs 1–5 crore would have only one vote. Under such a system, the largest firms – both foreign (via their captives) and the Indian software firms – have a number of advantages. First and most obviously, they have a vastly increased voting power over smaller firms. Second, it is far easier for large firms to organise and mobilise around selected candidates for the council. This is due to their smaller numbers and also closer interactions – socially, as much as through formal channels. In contrast, the smaller firms are dotted around the country and have very little interaction with each other. Third, given their vastly greater experience, much higher profile and deeper pockets, it is much easier for larger firms to run an election campaign amongst NASSCOM members than it would be for, say, a small data-entry firm from rural Punjab.

22. The 2011–13 Executive Council has more members from TNC captives than from domestic software services firms. More importantly, the three largest Giants – IBM, Accenture and EDS/HP – are all represented. See Appendices for the 2011–13 Executive Council.

23. Examining NASSCOM's Annual Reports from 2005 to 2009, the growing prominence of 'Destination India' in the association's agenda can be plotted: it goes from being the fifth point in NASSCOM's policy agenda in 2005/06 to being the first by 2008/09.

24. This resulted in invitations to NASSCOM to sit on committees across the entire Indian state apparatus. See Appendices for the links between NASSCOM and the Indian State Apparatus in 2010.

25. Writing in 2001, Shivanand Kanavi, a former high-ranking manager at TCS and CMC, observed that by the late 1990s Dewang Mehta, NASSCOM's chief executive, was referred to as the 'Minister of State for IT'. Moreover, Kanavi notes that this nickname was coined by the actual minister in charge of IT policy, Pramod Mahajan. And finally, Kavani claims the nickname was made only 'half-jokingly'. Indeed Kanavi goes on to note that 'Dewang and IT minister Pramod Mahajan have developed close ties, leading to easy access within the government for NASSCOM'; see Shivanand Kanavi, 'The Story of NASSCOM',

Business India, 19 February 2001, available at http://reflections-shivanand. blogspot.com/2008/01/story-of-nasscom.html (last accessed 19 July 2011).

26. This is best evidenced by NASSCOM's pressing for ITES to be taxed on the same generous terms as the software services industry in its 2006 Budget wish list.

27. NASSCOM warned the state that its reluctance on this issue would mean that TNCs would 'put on hold the transfer of more work to India' and might even consider 'migrating to other locations', and that India would 'lose up to $1 billion in revenues and sizeable employment generation'; see 'Government Urged to Amend IT Laws Relating to BPOs: $1 Billion at Stake, Warns NASSCOM', *Hindu Business Line*, 21 December 2005. NASSCOM also adopted a more subtle underlying strategy of winning support for concessions on ITES – it started to equate ITES with IT by breaking with convention and global awareness and referring to the industry in India as the IT-*ITES* industry (my emphasis). By putting the conceptually distinct IT and ITES together, it was better able to make the case for the same concessions on low-value ITES exports as for the higher-value IT exports.

28. Even in 2010/11 the contribution of the captives remained very low, at just over 15 per cent ($12.3 billion) of the industry's total revenues: see 'IT Sector to Post 18% Growth Next Fiscal', *Hindu*, 24 March 2011; also see Appendix G for the top offshore destinations for software services. The rankings, based on respected research by consultancy firm A.T. Kearney, show India to be the undisputed premier destination.

29. This is similar to the blocking thesis put forward to describe the City of London's ability, via the Bank of England, to pre-empt the state from intervening in the financial sector; see Ben Fine and Laurence Harris, *The Peculiarities of the British Economy* (London: Lawrence and Wishart, 1985).

30. NASSCOM's fawning over the contribution of TNC captives to the Indian software industry is captured perfectly in its report *Captives in India* (New Delhi: NASSCOM, 2010). The report included various platitudes on the TNC captives, including statements that they had 'evolved in their maturity', 'transformed themselves into centres of innovation', 'helped in spreading best practices in the location ecosystem', and even 'played a significant role in creating an innovation system in India'. Unfortunately, such praise was not substantiated with hard empirical evidence, raising questions over its rationale.

31. The scale of the Giants' expansion in India can be seen in the following statistics: IBM went from having 5,000 employees in India in 2002 to 73,000 in 2007, finally reaching an incredible 130,000 in 2010; Accenture went from 4,000 employees in 2003 to approximately 70,000 in 2011; and even Cap Gemini, the smallest of the Giants, employed 30,000 persons in India as of 2011. See www.ibm.in (last accessed 19 July 2011) for numbers of IBM's Indian employees from 2002 to 2007. However, after 2007 IBM stopped publishing numbers, claiming that, as it was a global company, the geographical distribution of its workforce had little meaning. This was most likely related to the fear of a backlash against it in the USA as unemployment in the country began to rise massively from 2008 onwards. The figure for IBM's Indian workforce in 2010 was available in 'IBM: India's Second Largest Private Sector Employer', *Times of India*, 18 August 2010. For Accenture employment data, see Dinesh Sharma, 'Accenture on Hiring Spree in India', *C-NET News*, 3 December 2003 (2003 figures) and Pranav Nambiar and Sujit John, 'India is at the Heart of Accenture

Ops', *Times of India*, 25 May 2011 (2011 figures). For the Cap Gemini figure, see Nambiar and John, 'India is at the Heart of Accenture Ops'.

32. After all, while being a poacher would save on costs of selection and training, being the victim of poaching would undermine the firm's ability to upgrade. This was because retaining employees was, according to Balaji Parthasarathy, vital to 'build up a repository of knowledge that would help in competing for subsequent, higher-end projects'; see Balaji Parthsarthy, 'Globalizing Information Technology: The Domestic Policy Context for India's Software Production and Exports', *Iterations: The Interdisciplinary Journal of Software History* 3, 2004. The anti-poaching agreements were mentioned in Bhaskar Vira, 'Working in the New Economy: The Labour Process in India's Call-Centre Industry', paper presented at Oxford University, 18 October 2007. The problem of attrition was raised as a question after the presentation. Dr Vira responded in detail about the implicit anti-poaching agreements established by the Indian Majors.

33. Why do TNCs have a superior ability to attract and retain talent? First and foremost, they pay higher salaries. As Professor Anthony D'Costa noted, in the Indian software industry 'the three top paymasters were all multinationals'; see Anthony D'Costa, *Exports, University–Industry Linkages and Innovation Challenges in Bangalore, India* (Washington, D.C.: World Bank, 2006): 16. Mridu Verma claims that IBM and Accenture pay 25–30 per cent higher than the Majors for employees at the same level – see Mridu Verma's, 'Infosys's Grand Strategy', ín B.V.S. Prasad and R. Puratchimni (eds), *The Rise of Indian MNCs: Insights and Experiences* (Hyderabad: Icfai, 2008): 43. TNCs can afford to do this as they can make each of their employees more productive than an employee of similar experience and education at a local firm. TNCs generally use superior technology and have better organisational capabilities. However, the TNC ability to attract the brightest and best in developing countries goes beyond mere remuneration, extending to the kudos attached to working for one of the world's largest corporations. There is also the possibility of moving permanently to the West, an incentive for some Indians (particular those from the lower middle class); working for a TNC is often referred to as 'a passport to the West'. Also, as the TNCs tend to be larger, the career opportunities available are more diverse.

34. Another factor would be the lack of need to poach; while the Giants were busily expanding in India during this period, this was primarily through mergers and acquisitions, meaning that the numbers of employees they were taking on at the time was not as great as in subsequent years.

35. For the Giants' initial graduate-level recruitment policies, see Ashok Desai, 'India', in Simon Commander (ed.), *The Software Industry in Emerging Markets* (Cheltenham: Edward Elgar, 2005).

36. Murali Patibandla and Bent Pedersen, 'The Role of Transnational Corporations in the Evolution of a High-Tech Industry: The Case of the Indian Software Industry – A Reply [to Athreye]', *World Development* 32(6), 2004.

37. Suma Athreye, 'The Role of Transnational Corporations in the Evolution of a High-Tech Industry: The Case of the Indian Software Industry – A Comment', *World Development*, 32(3), 2004.

38. Between 2001 and 2002, revenues from offshore work rose by 64 per cent whereas revenues from onsite work rose by just 7 per cent. See NASSCOM,

Software and Service Industry Performance FY02 (New Delhi: NASSCOM, 2002).

39. From *The Indian IT Industry NASSCOM Factsheet 2007* (New Delhi: NASSCOM, 2007). It is interesting to note that such an indicator was not released in the four subsequent factsheets. This may be because such rapid upgrading has not prevailed since.

40. See *Executive Summary: NASSCOM Annual Report 2005–06* (New Delhi: NASSCOM, 2006): 3.

41. Ibid.:3.

42. See Gubir Singh, 'IT is a Global Chartbuster', *Economic Times*, 16 October 2002.

43. The turn away from employing entry-level professionals and poaching senior managers has been put slightly earlier (that is, 2002–03) by some industry observers'; see Verma, 'Infosys's Grand Strategy': 139. There is also some disagreement as to the experience levels of those being poached. Some have argued it was employees with two to three years' experience; see Desai, 'India': 58. In contrast, others have argued that those poached included senior- and mid-level managers; see Verma, 'Infosys's Grand Strategy.

44. D. Wiggins, R. Datar, L. Leskela and P. Kumar, *Trends for the Indian and Chinese Software Industries*, Gartner Research Paper, 7 June 2003: 3.

45. Subir Roy, 'The Software Saga Should Continue', *Business Standard*, 23 July 2008.

46. See M. Giarratana, A. Pagano and S. Torrisi, 'The Role of Multinational Companies', in Ashish Arora and Alain Gambardella (eds), *From Underdogs to Tigers: The Rise and Growth of the Software Industry in Brazil, China, India and Ireland* (Oxford: Oxford University Press, 2005): 224.

CHAPTER 9

1. *The Information Technology Plan* (New Delhi: Government of India, 1998): 1.

2. Paul Baran, *The Political Economy of Growth* (New York: Monthly Review Press, 1962): xxix.

3. For a review of such studies, see Matthew McCartney's 'A Case of the Narrowing Discourse', in Alfredo Saad-Filho and Deborah Johnson (eds), *Neoliberalism: A Critical Reader* (London: Pluto Press, 2005).

4. See *NASSCOM Hosts the First Global Captive Conclave*, NASSCOM, 2011, available at www.nasscom.in (last accessed 19 July 2011).

5. See *Executive Summary: NASSCOM Annual Report 2008–09* (New Delhi: NASSCOM): 10. The number of members fell between December 2007 and December 2008 from 1,285 to 1,246 (the global economic downturn only began towards the end of this period). In December 2009, it had fallen to 1,235 members; *Executive Summary: NASSCOM Annual Report 2009–10* (New Delhi: NASSCOM): 11. In December 2010, the number of members had risen to 1,250; *Executive Summary: NASSCOM Annual Report 2010–11* (New Delhi: NASSCOM): 10.

6. See Section 10.2 for a full explanation of why software services firms from other developing countries will not be able to emulate the growth of the Indian Majors. It is telling that in a survey in which Indian software firms were asked to name the nationality of firms they see as their major rivals, 63 per cent of firms said US firms. Only 7 per cent saw firms from the Philippines

(the only developing country named) as competitors; see Tapan Choure and Yuvraj Shukla, *The Information Technology Industry in India* (Delhi: Kalpaz Publications, 2004): 129.

7. A British tabloid newspaper ran the headline 'Indian Call-Centre Axed for Burnley'; *Sun*, 4 July 2011. While the story discusses (in an admittedly light-hearted way) the trend of 'reshoring' of TNC captives, the underlying point is that the severity of wage inflation among workers in the IT industry in India has nullified the cost advantages previously enjoyed by Indian software SMEs over Western firms and by TNCs' captives in India over those in other locations.

8. For the Majors' contribution (47 per cent) to the industry's software exports, see Subir Roy, 'The Software Saga Should Continue', *Business Standard*, 23 July 2008. For the Majors' contribution (26 per cent) to the industry's overall revenues, see the OECD's *The ICT Sector in India: Performance, Growth and Key Challenges* (Paris: OECD, 2010): 41.

9. For example, between 2009 and 2011, attrition rates in Infosys rose from 13 per cent to 17 per cent; see Arindam Mukherjee, 'Is There Something Iffy in IT?', *Outlook India*, 2 May 2011. Similarly, attrition rates in Wipro during the same time period soared from just 12 per cent to an incredible 23 per cent; see Bhibu Rajan Mishra, 'Wipro Links Attrition to Pay Package', *Business Standard*, 19 June 2011.

10. According to NASSCOM, the rationale was proactive and 'to gain access to a diverse talent pool and expand their global footprint'; see *Impact of the IT–BPO Industry in India: A Decade in Review* (New Delhi: NASSCOM, 2010): 8. This complements comments from NASSCOM's president, Som Mittal, who has claimed that 'Indian companies have started hiring aggressively from different geographies to help them get closer to clients and get to know them better'; cited in Santanu Mishra, 'Indian IT Companies Yet to Outbid MNCs', *Economic Times*, 13 February 2009. This is not true. NASSCOM has been guilty of incorrectly equating the rationale behind establishment of offices and delivery centres in the USA and Western Europe (the first wave of FDI from the Indian majors) – to strengthen service capabilities in key markets by employing local persons with local knowledge – with the motivations behind the second wave of outward FDI from the Indian majors into China and Latin America. However, evidence suggests that the second wave was primarily intended to escape the feeder system within the Indian labour market by tapping into more stable labour markets. For example, there is little evidence to support the argument that outward FDI in Latin America and East Asia is to tap such markets – despite the surge of FDI from the Majors into Latin America and East Asia, the share of their export revenues derived from both Latin America and East Asia has remained stable. The share of industry revenues generated by sales to the emerging markets increased from 9.4 per cent in 2009 to 9.7 per cent in 2010; see *Information Technology Annual Report 2010–11* (New Delhi: NASSCOM): 2. Moreover, even the reports, statements and press releases by the Majors differentiate between delivery centres in the West and those in East Asia and Latin America. Like the delivery centres in India, those in East Asia and Latin America are referred to as global delivery centres, suggesting that their function is to service markets other than the one in which they are situated in. No such prefix is used for the Majors' delivery centres in the United States

or Western Europe, suggesting they are used to deliver service to the market in which they are situated.

11. Reasons for off-offshoring may vary. The factor which is most commonly cited for off-offshoring is the availability of cheaper labour elsewhere. However, thus far the primary factor for off-offshoring has been unsatisfactory service in the initial offshore location. This has led to off-offshoring back to the original location (also referred to as 'reshoring'). While reshoring has not yet become widespread, there have been a number of high-profile cases. In 2004, for example, Dell reshored their Indian call centres back to the USA following customer complaints.

12. While Indian Majors have expanded abroad, India remains the hub of their global operations.

13. This is already starting to happen. Captive call centres serving the US market have started moving from India to the Philippines. The stated rationale is not cost savings but a closer cultural affinity between Filipinos and Americans (attributed to the Philippines having been a US colony); see 'Call Centres in Philippines Employ More Agents than India', *Indian Express*, 18 July 2011. Jamaica and South Africa are attempting to lure TNCs away from India and to establish offshore call centres in their countries.

14. See the people skills and availability score from A.T. Kearney Global Services Location Index, available at www.atkearney.com/index.php/Publications/ offshoring-opportunities-amid-economic-turbulence-the-at-kearney-global-services-location-index-gsli-2011.html (last accessed 22 September 2011). India comes second after the USA. It is followed by China, the United Kingdom, Germany, Canada and France. Countries at a level of overall development comparable with India's cannot be compared with India in terms of people skills.

15. This was first adopted en masse by National Rail Enquiries in which callers phoning the enquiries line were no longer put straight through to a call centre but instead asked to press certain numbers on their phone according to the particular information they required. Most of these numbers would lead to voice recordings imparting the information. See Jon Snow, 'UK Call Centres: Crossroads of the Industry', *Journal of Property Investments and Finance* 23, 2010: 6, for an in-depth examination into this trend. The potential job losses from automation in the developed as well as developing world are immense.

16. Immigration in the West is usually discussed in terms of cheap labour (particularly prior to the 1970s), illegal immigration (a hot topic over the past decade), and refugees and asylum seekers. Such a discourse belies the huge scale of skilled migration, which oils the wheels of the global economy. An interesting article that explores skilled IT migration from India to the United States is Chris Fuller and Hari Narasimhan's article, 'From Landlords to Software Engineers: Migration and Urbanisation Amongst Tamil Brahmins', *Comparative Studies in Society and History* 50, 2008.

17. The Indian software firm CMC (now part of TCS) famously provided high-quality IT projects for the Indian government in the 1980s for a tenth of what a global giant would have charged; see Richard Heeks, *India's Software Industry: State Policy, Liberalisation and Industrial Development* (New Delhi: Sage, 1996): 276.

18. How do the Giants benefit from the current system? First, they clearly gain from the extension of concessions from IT service exports to ITES exports, as TNCs are predominantly engaged in export of ITES. Second, they benefit even

more from the state's inaction over their poaching, which not only generates for them huge cost savings on recruitment and training, but also serves to undermine the competitive challenge from their Indian rivals.

19. NASSCOM's annual reports highlight how its analysis of the labour market has evolved. In 2005 NASSCOM focused on the purely quantitative issue of shortages of software programmers. It stated that 'the availability of human resources remains by far the biggest challenge facing the sector'; see *Executive Summary: NASSCOM Annual Report 2005–06* (New Delhi: NASSCOM): 3. However, in 2008 it had gone one step further and accepted that employee attrition was a problem and talent retention was important; see *Executive Summary: NASSCOM Annual Report 2008–09* (New Delhi: NASSCOM): 14. However, it has never taken the final step of tying the problem of attrition to the practice of poaching. Indeed, only once in its entire history has NASSCOM acknowledged the poaching of employees, and even that was in a low-key 2010 committee report which advocated an unworkable self-regulatory approach. In more detail, the 2010 NASSCOM Committee on Ethics and Corporate Governance *urged* its members not to poach employees from other firms. Three recommendations were made. First, that employers should ask new employees for letters of consent from their former employers. Second, that an ombudsman should be appointed to address ethical concerns. And third, a tactic of whistle-blowing on poaching firms should be adopted by the industry. None has the capability to address the issue of poaching, which is based on asymmetries between firms in terms of ability to attract and retain talent.

20. The last time NASSCOM specifically identified the percentage of members that were TNCs was in 2003. It claimed that 20 per cent of NASSCOM members were TNC captives; see *Executive Summary: NASSCOM Annual Report 2003–04* (New Delhi: NASSCOM). Since then, NASSCOM's membership has been categorised by size of firm, location, and type of service, but not by whether the firm is Indian or not.

21. As stated by NASSCOM; available from www.nasscom.in (last accessed 19 August 2011).

22. Incredibly, the Emerge blog generates over 65,000 hits per month. This is possibly the strongest evidence that the managers of SMEs really do require advice and support on how to run their companies effectively and efficiently. The figure can be found in *Executive Summary: NASSCOM Annual Report 2008–09* (New Delhi: NASSCOM): 23.

23. See Choure and Shukla, *The Information Technology Industry in India*: 133, for a survey of Indian software firms regarding their key problems in the middle of the last decade. In the survey, 83 per cent of Indian software firms raised manpower shortages as one of the three major problems facing the industry, while 63 per cent included employee attrition. Interestingly, the two areas on which NASSCOM has focused – commercial infrastructure and physical infrastructure – were not deemed particularly problematic to the Indian firms in the survey. Only 23 per cent raised physical infrastructure as one of the three major problems facing them, while only 39 per cent included commercial infrastructure. Upon reading the various threads on the Emerge blogs, it becomes very noticeable that attrition, rather than manpower shortages per se, is now the biggest concern for Indian software SMEs.

24. Bread and circuses were used by the Roman elite to keep the masses content with their squalid life and deter them from making any attempt at redressing the huge inequalities of wealth.

25. This is despite Narayan Murthy's attempts at cultivating a 'cyber-geek' media persona. Such a persona has worked well for Bill Gates, whose key character traits are not his 'uber-cyber-geekiness' and technical wizardry but rather his extreme shrewdness, outstanding business acumen and total ruthlessness in suppressing any competition. Gates's projection of himself as a cyber-geek, now combined with an avuncular kind-heartedness (through his charity foundation), has helped some of Microsoft's business practices to fly under the media radar.

26. Narayan Murthy and Azim Premji, like all wise capitalists, rarely miss a chance to denigrate the previous dirigiste regime and speak of the evils of state intervention, while simultaneously taking full advantage of the state's largesse in their own industry. Narayan Murthy even managed to launch an attack on the ISI period in a speech commemorating Netaji, an Indian independence leader of statist and leftist persuasions; cited in 'Netaji Could Have Taken Us past China: Murthy', *Times of India*, 24 January 2011.

27. For example, NASSCOM's one investigation into poaching – the 2010 NASSCOM Committee on Ethics and Corporate Governance – was chaired by Narayan Murthy, founder of Infosys and the most high-profile of the Major's representatives. This may be the start of a more assertive campaign by the Majors to address the issue of poaching.

28. The state's acquiescence in various IT policies recommended by NASSCOM was based on these policies not running counter to wider, deeper and more powerful interests.

29. In the USA, Adobe, Apple and Google have engaged in anti-poaching agreements; for more details, see Stephanie Kirchgaessner, 'Tech Firms Agree to Halt Anti-Poaching Deals', *Financial Times*, 25 September 2010.

30. If the Majors reach the size of the Giants, anti-poaching agreements will easily be established, as the asymmetries in talent attraction and retention will narrow if not disappear entirely. In the more immediate term, Wipro has tied the pay packages of its senior managers to their ability to lessen attrition; see Bhibu Rajan Mishra, 'Wipro Links attrition to Pay Package', *Business Standard*, 19 June 2011.

31. Indian software Majors lack experience in greenfield application development, which requires very deep domain knowledge; see Santanu Mishra, 'Indian IT Companies Yet to Outbid MNCs', *Economic Times*, 13 February 2009. Government procurement would provide opportunities for such firms to gain experience. Unfortunately, the Indian state has of late been awarding its high-end IT systems contracts to the Global Giants. The Reserve Bank of India's IT systems upgrade went to IBM. This could have provided one or more Indian Majors with a valuable learning experience in IT consultancy. Instead, the Indian state's procurement has helped propel IBM to the dominant position it now holds within the Indian market; see 'IBM in India', available at www. ibm.com/news/in/en/2008/01/23/v141107r67598o89.html (last accessed 19 July 2011).

32. Former software public-sector undertaking (PSU) CMC provided software services to the Indian state at a tenth of what a global giant would have charged; see Heeks, *India's Software Industry*: 276.

33. CMC provided a whole array of IT infrastructure projects for the Indian government in the 1980s. Using this experience, it then went on to win a number of foreign contracts, including to design the software for the London Underground and Penang Port. Two of the most accomplished scholars working on the Indian software industry have argued that the domestic market can and should act as a springboard for software export success; see A. Parasarathi and K. Joseph, 'Innovation under Export Orientation', in Anthony D'Costa and E. Sridharan (eds), *India in the Global Software Industry: Innovation, Firm Strategies and Development* (Basingstoke: Palgrave Macmillan, 2004). A similar argument has been made for Indian industries in general; see Nagesh Kumar, 'India: Industrialisation, Liberalisation, and Inward and Outward Foreign Direct Investment', in John Dunning and R. Narula (eds), *Foreign Direct Investment and Government: Catalysts for Economic Restructuring* (London: Routledge, 1995).

34. For a more detailed discussion of the benefits of evading TNC competition in the software services industry in order to experiment with new business models, see Suma Athreye, 'The Role of Transnational Corporations in the Evolution of a High-Tech Industry: The Case of the Indian Software Industry – A Comment', *World Development* 32(3), 2005.

35. There is much disagreement over which markets offer the best prospects. Many believe Indian software firms should seek to penetrate the East Asian countries. Professor Anthony D'Costa believes the best opportunity lies in the Japanese market; see Anthony D'Costa, *Exports, University–Industry Linkages and Innovation Challenges in Bangalore, India* (Washington, D.C.: World Bank, 2006): 20–1. In contrast, Dr Durgesh Rai perceives Taiwan as providing excellent growth prospects for Indian software companies, opening up the possibility of solid linkages between Taiwanese hardware and Indian software industries; see Durgesh Rai, 'Patterns and Structure of the Indian IT Industry: Scope for Strengthening India–Taiwan Ties', in *Proceedings of Advancing Regional Economic Integration: Potential Roles of India and Taiwan*, 25th Pacific Economic Community Seminar, 2 December 2010, Chinese Taipei Pacific Economic Cooperation Committee. Gartner, the British consultancy firm, believes that the Chinese market offers Indian software firms particularly rich rewards; see D. Wiggins, R. Datar, L. Leskela and P. Kumar, *Trends for the Indian and Chinese Software Industries*, Gartner Research Paper, 7 June 2003. However, while East Asia appears to have captured the observers' attention, the developing world might provide better long-term growth prospects, owing to the software services market being in its infancy there at the moment, plus the near total absence of local firms able to provide even basic IT services, and the total eschewal of such markets by the Giants (except for the largest government IT systems projects).

36. It is generally accepted that Indian software firms have certain advantages over the Giants in both the East Asian market (due to cultural similarities in deference for hierarchy, etc.) and other parts of the developing world (related to comparable levels of overall economic development, and therefore demand for similar types of services as those offered in the Indian market). Former government economist Ashok Desai postulates that the best trading partners for India are the Indian Ocean developing countries, owing to their long history of economic interaction, and strong cultural affinities, with India. Moreover, Desai argues that the significant populations of ethnic Indians in many such countries

would help to form a commercial bridge; see Ashok Desai, 'Renovating Our Image: The Indian Ocean Countries Are Our Best Trade Partners', available at www.ashokdesai.blogspot.com (last accessed 31 August 2011).

37. There is a definite role for government. This is because presently the Giants, rather than the Majors, are providing software services to the largest non-IT-related Indian corporations. Prominent examples of this include Accenture's provision of IT infrastructure and application management services to Dabur (India's Proctor and Gamble) whereas IBM provides the IT requirements to India's largest telecommunications provider, Bharti. Had such contracts gone to Indian Majors instead of the Giants, not only would they have boosted the former's market share, they would have provided substantial learning opportunities.

CHAPTER 10

1. See Karl Marx, *The German Ideology* (London: Prometheus Books, 1998).
2. The first report on the IT industry in India for the International Development agencies was Nagy Hanna's *Exploiting Information Technology for Development: The Case of India* (Washington, D.C.: World Bank, 1994). In the foreword, Harold Messenger, the director of the World Bank's Asia Technical Department, noted that while the report was primarily for the Indian government, the findings would be 'of wide interest to other countries'. This was prescient, as all following World Bank reports on the Indian IT industry were primarily directed at influencing the policy agendas of other developing countries.
3. It is sub-Saharan Africa where the World Bank has been particularly active in promoting the emulation of the Indian software services industry. In 2009/10 it organised a 'learning visit' for African policymakers to Indian IT hubs as well as a follow-up conference titled 'Skills for ICT: A South–South Experience Exchange between India and Africa', though the exchange was only in one direction. More information on this 'exchange' is available at www.worldbank. org/.
4. The World Bank-affiliated International Finance Corporation has gone so far as to claim that the Indian software services model might allow developing countries to 'leapfrog' the manufacturing stage of development. See Robert Miller, *Leapfrogging? India's Information Technology Industry and the Internet* (Washington, D.C.: World Bank, 2001).
5. To quote Miller: 'Software exports, the earliest harbinger of a more widespread IT expansion, began only in 1985, when Texas Instruments established its subsidiary in Bangalore'; see ibid.: 15. As Part 2 has shown, this is completely incorrect. Software exports had begun over a decade before TI's investment in India.
6. Some industry commentators believe that TI's software development centre in Bangalore provided a demonstration effect to other TNCs and Indian software firms of the potential of service provision by remote delivery, which in turn triggered the influx of IT-related FDI into India; see Suma Athreye, 'The Role of Transnational Corporations in the Evolution of a High-Tech Industry: The Case of India's Software Industry – A Comment', *World Development*, 32(3), 2004. This is not true. In the ten years following TI's establishment of its captive in Bangalore, only a small number of TNCs had adopted a model in which services were provided by remote delivery from India. A far more credible explanation

would be that the growth of the Indian Majors during the 1990s proved the feasibility of the remote delivery model. Moreover, it was the success of Indian BPO firm Daksh between 2000 and 2004 in providing call-centre support to Amazon that prompted other TNCs to consider, for the first time, establishing their own call centres in India. Prior to that, the few TNC captives in India involved in BPO had focused on back-office operations rather than front-desk ones.

7. The TI investment in Bangalore is often attributed to an NRI member of the TI board recommending and then pushing for India as an offshore software development base. More broadly, from the late 1960s onward highly technically skilled Indians have entered the US economy, many of them reaching highly influential positions across corporate America, but particularly in high-tech industries. It is conceivable that this may have created a perception that India would be a suitable location for establishing IT-related captives. This is not the same as saying the Indian diaspora was the cause of the Indian software industry, a myth dissected in the book's Primer.

8. A few notable exceptions include Intel, GE and Microsoft, who have set up their largest non-US-based R&D labs in India.

9. The states in India with IT hubs, such as Karnataka and Andhra Pradesh, also tend to adopt the expensive Microsoft packages in state schools and departments. In contrast, states not yet penetrated by IT hubs have tended to adopt Linux, like most other developing countries. This suggests that the IT industry has exerted some influence on government institutions – perhaps subliminally, perhaps more explicitly – persuading them to adopt expensive Microsoft packages rather than the free alternatives. See Myth 7 in the book's Primer for a more detailed presentation of this argument.

10. The World Bank's 2008 Knowledge Economy Index (KEI), available at www.siteresources.worldbank.org.

11. For a detailed exposition see A. and V.N. Balasubramanyam, 'International Trade in Services: The Case of India's Computer Software Industry', *World Economy* 20(6), 2006.

12. The only reason Indian software firms still exist is due to the development 'head start' they had prior to the influx of captives. It is likely in other developing countries that lack more established indigenous software firms the effects of an FDI influx will be catastrophic. A fledgling software industry will go the same way as did the Indian BPO firms in the early 2000s – the more successful were acquired by either the Giants or the Majors, while the rest were forced out of the industry. As already noted in Chapter 9, such a scenario is now emerging amongst Indian software firms.

13. 'Race to the bottom' refers to the competition between countries or locations within them to attract capital via various inducements and incentives. The end result is that all the countries become progressively worse off as they undercut each other via tax concessions, removal of pro-labour laws, etc., in an increasingly desperate bid to attract foreign capital.

14. Professor Sumantra Ghoshal of London Business School, speaking at the NASSCOM IT Fair in Mumbai in 2001, noted that only Indian software services firms, and even then primarily the largest ones, were engaged in such markets. 'What looked like global competition was,' he stated, 'actually local [Indian] competition. Infosys, Wipro and TCS were competing with each other on the same ground'; cited in 'Indian Companies Need to Build Human Capital:

Ghoshal', *Rediff*, 19 February 2001, available at www.rediff.com (last accessed 19 July 2011).

15. For a chart illustrating the exponential growth of the global software market from the late 1970s onwards, see Richard Heeks, *India's Software Industry: State Policy, Liberalisation and Industrial Development*: 109.

16. Some of the Giants, such as EDS, were involved in IT outsourcing, but this had become a sideshow to their core focus on higher-end IT consulting and IT services, in which the profit margins were much higher.

17. The boon that was the absence of Giant competition in the lower-end software services market the Indian software firms were serving in the late 1980s and 1990s has been discussed by Athreye in 'The Role of Transnational Corporations in the Evolution of a High-Tech Industry'.

18. Terry Byres, professor emeritus at the University of London, has stated that the mainstream portrayal of the Indian state is one of a ' Kafkaesque insect'; cited in Terence Byres (ed.), *The State, Development Planning and Liberalisation in India* (Oxford: Oxford University Press, 1997): 14.

19. Examples abound. Machine tools and aluminium ingots were notable successes in the early days of the ISI period. A more recent and higher-profile industry to have benefitted from state intervention prior to 1991 has been Indian pharmaceuticals. Bijal Barnwal notes that this industry 'made impressive progress in the 1970s and 1980s largely as a consequence of focused policy level intervention'; see Bijay Barnwal, *Economics Reforms and Policy Change: A Case Study of the Indian Drug Industry* (New Delhi: Classical Publishing House, 2000): 99. Another example is the Indian automobile industry, which also benefitted from substantial and effective state intervention; see Deepak Narayana, *The Motor Vehicle Industry in India: Growth within a Regulatory Policy Environment* (New Delhi: IBH Publishing Co., 1989).

20. See Dani Rodrik and Arvind Subramanium, *From Hindu Growth to Productivity Surge: The Mystery of the Indian Growth Transition*, IMF Staff Papers, 2004.

21. This is in contrast to the experiences of former communist countries, in which economic growth was greatest when the drag exerted by the state sector was least; see ibid.: 18.

22. See Atul Kohli, *Democracy and Development in India: From Socialism to Pro-Business* (Oxford: Oxford University Press, 2010).

23. See Richard Herring, 'Embedded Particularism: India's Failed Developmental State', in Meredith Woo-Cummings (ed.), *The Developmental State* (Ithaca, N.Y.: Cornell University Press, 2004).

24. It remains to be seen how the 2011 anti-corruption movement in India plays out. The key point is whether it will continue to focus on low-to-mid-tier corruption or evolve into a broader social movement which tackles the broader questions regarding the legitimacy of, and justification for, the current economic regime in India.

25. For an excellent analysis of the Indian government's position at the WTO with regard to pursuing the agenda set out by NASSCOM, see Jayati Ghosh, 'The Political Economy of Self-Delusion', *Macroscan*, 2006, available at www.macroscan.com (last accessed 19 July 2011).

26. Two articles discuss this situation, but from different perspectives. From the Indian perspective, see G. Ganpathy Subramaniam and M.K. Venu, 'India Demands 195k H1-B Visas', *Economic Times*, 24 June 2005. From the US perspective, see Paul McDougall, 'American IT Jobs Give Bush a Valuable

Bargaining Chip in Talks with India', *Information Week*, 28 February 2006. These negotiations have since taken a back seat as a result of the global economic downturn. However, it is likely that such demands will resume once an upswing occurs.

27.   The employment figures for the industry were cited in Durgesh Rai, 'Patterns and Structure of the Indian IT Industry: Scope for Strengthening India–Taiwan Ties', in *Proceedings of Advancing Regional Economic Integration: Potential Roles of India and Taiwan*, 25th Pacific Economic Community Seminar, 2 December 2010, Chinese Taipei Pacific Economic Cooperation Committee. To put the software services industry's employment figures into context, 225 million Indians work in the agricultural sector, just under 50 per cent of the country's labour force. Even Indian industry employs over 80 million workers, 25 million of which are in the formal economy; data from *The India Labour Market Report 2008* (Mumbai: Tata Institute of Social Sciences): 11.

28.   Using the conservative estimate from the CIA World Fact Book of the total Indian labour force as constituting 478 million people. With a looser definition of 'labour', the population of the labour force would rise significantly and the percentage share of the labour force employed by the software industry would drop correspondingly.

29.   See 'Top Ten Companies That Bagged H1-B Visas', *Rediff*, 18 December 2009, available at www.rediff.com (last accessed 19 July 2011).

CHAPTER 11

1.   Michael Barratt-Brown, *Models of Political Economy* (London: Penguin, 1984): 193.
2.   Karl Marx, *Eighteenth Brumaire of Louis Bonaparte* (London: CreateSpace, 2011): 1.

Appendices

APPENDIX A

The Software Industry in India, by Type of Firm
(with special reference to the software services firms)

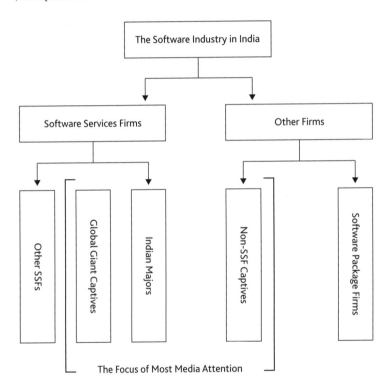

APPENDIX B

IT Policy Formulation According to the Developmental Department Literature

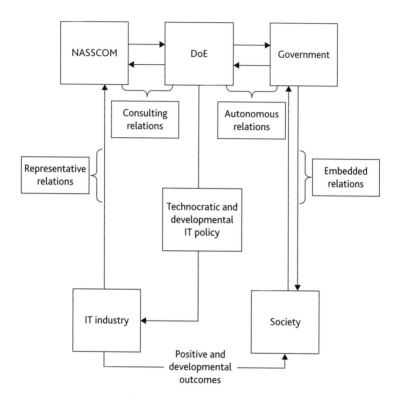

APPENDIX C

The Internal Power Structure of NASSCOM

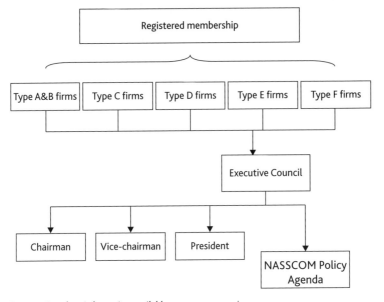

Source: Based on information available at www.nasscom.in

Firm type	Size of firm (gross revenue from IT software and services in Rs crore)	Votes per firm
A	Exceeding 500	6
B	200–500	6
C	50–200	4
D	20–50	3
E	5–20	2
F	1–5	1

APPENDIX D

NASSCOM Executive Council, 2011–13

Firm	Type of Firm
Accenture	Captive (US)
Aegis	Captive (UK)
Apollo Health	Domestic non-software services
Bharti Airtel	Domestic non-software services
BT	Captive (UK)
Cognizant	Indo-US joint venture software services
CRISIL	Domestic non-software services
Dell	Captive (US)
Google	Captive (US)
Headstrong	Captive (US)
HP	Captive (US)
IBM	Captive (US)
IBS	Captive (Russia)
Infosys	Domestic software services
Infotech	Domestic software services
Larsen and Toubro Infotech	Domestic software services
Make My Trip	Indian non-software services
Microsoft	Captive (US)
Mindtree	Indo-US joint venture software services
Movico	Captive (The Netherlands)
Persistent	Domestic software services
Quattro BPO	Domestic software services
Satayam	Domestic software services
TCS	Domestic software services
Wipro	Domestic software services

Source: Based on data from www.nasscom.in

APPENDIX E

NASSCOM and the Indian State Apparatus, 2010

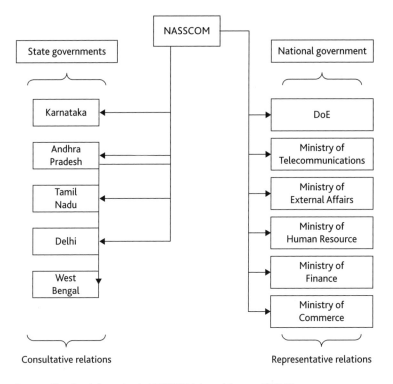

Source: Based on information in NASSCOM Annual Reports 2005–10.

Notes: The term 'representative relations' is used to denote that NASSCOM has its own representatives sitting on one or more committees of the connected ministry. The term 'consultative relations' refers to NASSCOM's role as strategic consultant on IT matters.

APPENDIX F

Priority Issues for Firms, NASSCOM and the State

Priority Issues for TNC Captives	Priority Issues for Indian Software Firms	Priority Issues for NASSCOM	Priority Issues for the Indian State
Tax concessions	Employee attrition	Physical infrastructure/visas	Physical infrastructure
Physical infrastructure	Manpower/skills shortage	Tax concessions	Tax concessions
Data security and software piracy	Commercial infrastructure	Data security and software piracy	Data security and software piracy
Political stability	Access to finance	Manpower/skills shortage	Manpower/skills shortage

Sources: For TNC priorities in India, adapted from Gartner Research Ratings in Mark Kobayashi-Hillary, *Outsourcing to India: The Offshore Advantage* (New York: Springer, 2004): 141. For Indian software service firms, adapted from CMU Survey in Tapan Choure and Yuvraj Shukla, *The Information Technology Industry in India* (Delhi: Kalpaz Publications, 2004): 133. For NASSCOM, adapted from information available at www.nasscom.in. For the Indian State, adapted from information available at www.mit.gov.in.

APPENDIX G

Top Offshore Destinations for Software Services

Rank	Country	Financial Attractiveness	People Skills	Business Environment	Total Score
1	India	3.11	2.76	1.14	7.01
2	China	2.62	2.55	1.31	6.49
3	Malaysia	2.78	1.38	1.83	5.99
4	Egypt	3.1	1.36	1.35	5.81
5	Indonesia	3.24	1.53	1.01	5.78
9	Philippines	3.18	1.31	1.16	5.65
28	Pakistan	3.23	1.16	0.76	5.15
33	Jamaica	2.81	0.86	1.34	5.01
45	South Africa	2.27	0.93	1.37	4.57

Source: A.T. Kearney Global Services Location Index, 2011. The weight distribution for the three categories is 40:30:30. The scale for the three categories is 0-4: 0-3: 0-3. Available at www.atkearney.com/index.php/Publications/offshoring-opportunities-amid-economic-turbulence-the-at-kearney-global-services-location-index-gsli-2011.html (last accessed 28 September 2011).

Index